Soul Vegetarian Cookbook

Published by
Communicators Press
P.O. Box 26063, Washington, D.C. 20001
(202) 726-8618
FAX (202) 291-9149

Copyright © 1992, Communicators Press

All rights reserved. No part of this book may be reproduced or
transmitted in any form or by any means, electronic or mechanical,
including photocopying, recording, or by any information storage and
retrieval system, without permission in writing from the Publisher.

ISBN 0-9620463-4-5

The scriptural references used in this book are taken
from the New Scofield Reference Bible

Dedication

A special tribute is extended to **Sister Karliyah Baht Israel,** nutritionist, devoted and dedicated pioneer, mother, sister and teacher who has contributed greatly to the creation and perfection of vegetarian nutrition.

The Soul Vegetarian Cookbook is dedicated to all those brothers and sisters who have struggled throughout the years to make this information available for those who are seeking a new way of life through diet.

We recommend that you use high quality, natural products to ensure that your recipes meet the high standards and optimum taste we have set for each dish.

The Soul Vegetarian Cookbook is your doorway to excellent health, good eating and longevity. All the way from Northeast Africa, Jerusalem, we continue to spread a positive image of the proper nutritional intake in order to maintain a complete and balanced diet, which builds strong, healthy bodies.

"It is wealth when you have your health."

To you, we give an alternative diet that has been tested and proven to be a creative and healthful awakening for vegetarians as well as non-vegetarians across the globe.

Bon Appetite!

B'tayah-vone!

To your health!

Table Of Contents

Introduction 1

What Is A Nutrition Room? 2

Helpful Cooking Hints 3

Healthful Substitutes for the New Vegetarian 5

Handy Recipe Measurement Conversion Table 6

FOOD SECTIONS

Breads 9

Sauces and Gravies 15

Soups 23

Main Dishes 31

Raw Dishes 57

Easy Sprouting 67

Salad Dressings, Dips and Relishes 69

Desserts 79

Beverages 95

Suggested Menus 99

Important Food Supplements
    Needed For A Balanced Diet 101

Introduction

There are many reasons why we offer you the *Soul Vegetarian Cookbook*, but our main purpose is to direct you toward a totally **new** way of eating.

Diet is a very important factor for the survival of a people. A good diet is based upon the organic elements that give and sustain life. Many people take the human body and its functions lightly. They do not consider what they consume as having a direct and permanent effect on the quality of their health. That is why we take this time to present a consciousness and seriousness about the diet-related diseases that are destroying our people by the thousands each year. Cancer, hypertension, arteriosclerosis, sugar diabetes and strokes are just a few diseases that we can lessen the effects of, or even eradicate, by adopting a proper diet.

The most common and serious diseases are caused by incorrect eating and drinking. If not properly prepared, food will not furnish life-force but will disrupt the cycles of the body. Current statistics are really heartbreaking (no pun intended); cancer cases in the U.S. were estimated at 1,010,000 for 1989.* At least 850,000 people have been struck by colon-rectal cancer alone. Medical research has definitely established the link between colon-rectal cancer and meat eating. It is a long established fact (whether admitted to or not) that the body and digestive system is not equipped to break down the fibers that meat contains. Let's face it -- the eating of animals is just no preparation for long life. It is not possible for a healthy mind and body to function in harmony without natural dietary habits. **"You are what you eat."**

The recipes in the *Soul Vegetarian Cookbook* are all-natural, white sugar-free and white flour-free, non-diary and free of animal by-products. Yet, your taste buds will still remain satisfied. It will be difficult for you to believe that these dishes utilize only nuts, grains, seeds, whole wheat flour, soy beans and their complimentary natural ingredients. You will be amazed at the creativity displayed in these life-giving, life-sustaining dishes and menus.

*American Cancer Society Statistics

What Is A Nutrition Room?

A nutrition room is the part of the home set aside for the planning and preparation of nutritional foods that will sustain and maintain the good health of the family.

With this definition in mind, we invite you to step through the door of our nutrition room. From here, you will embark on a journey that will lay before you a totally new experience within the realm of vegetarian cuisine.

For the past 22 years, we have concentrated on developing the skills and perfecting the methods which make the vegetarian diet nutritious, attractive and delicious. We believe we have achieved those goals. However, the final determination is up to you. These recipes are road maps to eternal life. Please follow them carefully and enjoy the journey.

Helpful Cooking Hints

1. A good cook must have these three important qualities:
   a. willing spirit
   b. consistency
   c. cleanliness

2. Use long-grain rice. It cooks fluffier and has a tendency not to be as starchy.

3. Food which is three days old or older should not be used because either it has spoiled or has acquired a refrigerator taste. This procedure helps you to avoid unhealthy incidents.

4. Make breakfast and lunch your heaviest meals. Eating heavy at a late hour can cause weight-gain and stomach discomforts.

5. Avoid peeling vegetables unless absolutely necessary because many nutrients are found in the peelings.

6. You will use less spices when cooking at a medium-to-low flame because at that temperature, the spices cook through the food.

7. Recipes utilizing pickle relish should use the liquid from the relish to enhance the flavor.

8. When adding salt or tamari sauce, add a little at a time to the recipe, tasting after each measurement to ensure that dishes are not too salty.

9. At certain times, vegetables and fruits can be bitter. It is a good practice to know whether the vegetables and fruits are in season.

10. In recipes that call for margarine, use soy margarine or vegetable oil margarine.

11. When making cakes, use no-salt margarine because salted margarine leaves a slightly salty flavor in cakes and cookies.

12. All fruits and vegetables must be washed and rinsed before use.

13. Even though these recipes are perfectly measured, experienced cooks can add ingredients according to taste.

14. Serve rice with chickpeas or soybeans. It gives you a complete protein meal.

15. Always soak your beans for 24 hours before using them. This releases harmful enzymes that cause gas and shortens the cooking process. Cover with 3" of water over beans.

16. "Clabbered milk" is slightly soured or curdled soy milk.

17. "Clabbered pulp" is the grainy substance remaining from homemade soy milk after straining that has slightly soured, used as a natural "rising" for cakes, cookies, etc.

18. Pasta cooked *al dente* is done but firm.

19. Read the label on all food packages that you purchase. Beware of artificial colorings, preservatives and additives.

Healthful Substitutes For The New Vegetarian

Instead Of:	Use:
Vinegar	Lemon
1 Tsp. Baking Powder	1/2 C. Clabbered Soy Milk
1 C. Granulated Sugar	1 C. Brown Sugar or
	2 C. Sifted Powdered Brown Sugar
1 C. Honey	1 1/4 C. Brown Sugar + 1/4 C. Liquid
1 C. Buttermilk	1 Tbsp. Lemon Juice +
	Soy Milk To Make 1 Cup,
	Let Stand For 5 Minutes.
1/8 Tsp. Garlic Powder	1 Clove Fresh Garlic
1 Tbsp. Cornstarch	2 Tbsp. Whole Wheat Flour
1/2 C. Tomato Sauce + 1/2 C. Water	1 C. Tomato Juice
Fats, Hard Melted	Cold Pressed Oil or Coconut Butter
Coffee	Soy Coffee *(See recipe pg. 87)*
Cocoa	Carob Powder
Chocolate (1 Sq. Oz.)	3-4 Tbsp. Carob + 1 Tbsp. Oil
	2 Tbsp. Liquid
Jello	Agar-Agar
Soft	1 Tbsp. Flakes + 2 C. Liquid
Firm	1 Tbsp. Granulated + 3 1/4 C. Liquid
	or 2 Tbsp. Flakes + 3 1/4 C. Liquid
Butter Or Margarine	Soy Margarine or 7/8 C. Oil +
	1/2 Tsp. Salt
Sour Milk (For Baking)	1 C. Sweet Soy Milk +
	2 Tsp. Lemon Juice,
	3/4 Tsp. Cream Of Tartar
Brown Sugar	Raw Or Date Sugar
Egg Whites For Merangues	Flax Jell Whipped *(See recipe below)*

Flax Seed Jell

Ingredients: 5 Tbsp. Flax Seed and 5 C. Cold Water

Soak seeds in water for one hour. Simmer for twenty minutes. Set in refrigerator. Beat as you would egg whites.

Good **only** in raw recipes or folded in jello. **Will not hold form in recipes that involve cooking.**

Handy Recipe Measurement Conversion Table

Kitchen Math With Metric Table

MEASURE	EQUIVALENT	METRIC (ML)
1 Tbsp.	3 tsp.	14.8 milliliters
2 Tbsp.	1 oz.	29.6 milliliters
1 jigger	1 1/2 oz.	44.4 milliliters
1/4 cup	4 Tbsp.	59.2 milliliters
1/3 cup	5 Tbsp. plus 1 tsp.	78.9 milliliters
1/2 cup	8 Tbsp.	118.4 milliliters
1 cup	16 Tbsp.	236.8 milliliters
1 pint	2 cups	473.6 milliliters
1 quart	4 cups	947.2 milliliters
1 liter	4 cups plus 3 1/2 Tbsp.	1,000.0 milliliters
1 oz. (dry)	2 Tbsp.	28.35 grams
1 pound	16 oz.	453.59 grams
2.21 pounds	35.3 oz.	1.00 kilogram

The Approximate Conversion Factors For Units Of Volume

To Convert From	To	Multiply By
teaspoons (tsp.)	milliliters (ml)	5
tablespoons (Tbsp.)	milliliters (ml)	15
fluid ounces (fl. oz.)	milliliters (ml)	30
cups (c)	liters (l)	0.24
pints (pt.)	liters (l)	0.47
quarts (qt.)	liters (l)	0.95
gallons (gal.)	liters (l)	3.8
milliliters (ml)	fluid ounces (fl. oz.)	0.03
liters (l)	pints (pt.)	2.1
liters (1)	quarts (qts.)	1.06
liters (1)	gallons (gal.)	0.26

SIMPLIFIED MEASURES

dash = less than 1/8 teaspoon   2 pt. (4 c.) = 1 qt.
3 tsp. = 1 Tbsp.   4 qt. (liquid) = 1 gal.
16 Tbsp. = 1 cup   8 qt. (solid) - 1 peck
1 cup = 1/2 pt.   4 pecks = 1 bushel
2 cups = 1 pt.   16 oz. = 1 lb.

If you want to measure part-cups by the tablespoon, remember:

4 Tbsp. = 1/4 cup   10 2/3 Tbsp. = 2/3 cup
5 1/3 Tbsp. = 1/3 cup   12 Tbsp. = 3/4 cup
8 Tbsp. = 1/2 cup   14 Tbsp. = 7/8 cup

BREADS

Loaf Bread

Garlic Bread

Rye Bread

Onion Bread

Cornbread

Cornbread Patties

Pancakes

Whole-wheat Cheese Toast

Homemade Biscuits

Crackers

Whole Wheat Flour Batter

"It is written that it is not by bread alone that one can live, but by every word which proceeds from the mouth of God."

Matthew 4:4

Breads

LOAF BREAD

1 lb. whole wheat flour
1/2 stick margarine
10 oz. soy milk (clabbered)
   (see recipe, pg. 96)
(see Helpful Cooking Hints)

1. Sift flour into large mixing bowl. Add margarine and mix well.
2. Add milk and make soft dough. Knead for approximately 20 minutes.
3. Place dough in greased loaf pan and place in warm area (not oven). Let rise until dough is twice its original size.
4. Bake for 30 minutes or until golden brown and bread comes away from sides of pan. Insert knife to test. If dough sticks, bake for 10-15 minutes longer. Dough can be shaped into dinner rolls.

Yields: One 9 X 5 Inch Loaf

GARLIC BREAD

Use recipe for loaf bread. Blend fresh garlic with clabbered soy milk *or* add 1 tbsp. of garlic powder.

RYE BREAD

Use recipe for loaf bread. Add 1/4 cup rye (raw, clean) to mixture.

ONION BREAD

Use recipe for loaf bread. Add 1/2 cup dried onions.

CORNBREAD

4 cups yellow corn meal
1/2 cup whole wheat flour
1/2 cup wheat germ
3 cups warm water
1/2 tsp. salt

1 1/2 sticks margarine
1/3 cup vegetable oil
1 cup honey
1 cup fresh clabbered milk

1. Melt margarine and oil together.
2. Mix all dry ingredients, then add honey.
3. Add warm water; clabbered milk and mix very well.
4. Pour in greased pan.
5. Bake at 425 degrees for 30-35 minutes.
   Yields: 14 Servings

CORNBREAD PATTIES

1 cup corn meal
1/4 stick margarine
2 tbsp. vegetable oil
1/4 cup soy flour

1/4 cup whole wheat flour
salt (to taste)
1 tbsp. brown sugar
2 tbsp. wheat germ
3/4 cup water

1. Mix dry ingredients well.
2. Add water, forming a batter of stiff consistency. Stir in sugar and margarine.
3. Heat oil in pan until hot. Pour oil into batter and stir.
4. Drop batter by the tablespoonsful into a lightly oiled skillet. (Three to four will fit in a medium skillet.)
5. Let cook until patties dry out on top side.
6. Turn over and let brown. Serve immediately.
   Yields: 4 Servings

Breads

PANCAKES

3 cups whole wheat flour
3 cups wheat germ flakes
1/4 cup bran
1/4 cup honey
3 tsp. vanilla
2 cups soy milk
(see recipe, pg. 96)
1/3 cup vegetable oil

Yields: 15 Large Pancakes

1. With wire wisk, mix all dry ingredients well.
2. Add vanilla, honey, and soy milk and mix well. Add more soy milk if necessary to desired consistency.
3. Cook on lightly oiled skillet or on grill.
4. When using this batter for waffles, add 1/2 cup oatmeal.

WHOLE-WHEAT CHEESE TOAST

1 tbsp. soy cheese
(see recipe, pg. 73)
2 slices whole wheat bread
1/3 stick margarine

Yields: 1 Serving

1. Spread soy cheese on whole wheat bread.
2. Brown in skillet with margarine.

HOMEMADE BISCUITS

1 lb. whole wheat flour
1 tsp. vege salt

3 sticks margarine
1/4 cup wheat germ

clabbered soy pulp (from one day old soy milk)
(See Helpful Cooking Hints and recipe, pg. 96)

1. Mix whole wheat flour and margarine with a fork.
2. Add wheat germ and mix well.
3. Mix in clabbered soy pulp well until dough is soft and wet.
4. Drop biscuits on greased cookie sheet. Place in hot oven at 350 degrees for 20 minutes. Serve hot.

Yields: 10-12 Servings

CRACKERS

1 lb. whole wheat flour
3 sticks margarine
1 cup clean, raw sesame seeds
1 1/2 cups water
1/3 cup oil

Yields: 50 Crackers

Sift flour once. Add oil, margarine and sesame seeds to a half pound of flour. Add water and mix well. Do not knead. Roll them out thin and cut into desired shapes. Place in baking pan and bake for 10 minutes in hot oven at 350 degrees.

WHOLE WHEAT FLOUR BATTER
(WET AND DRY)

Instead of deep-frying our foods we use less oils with the batters. Normally we suggest using the dry batter but for extra coating and flavor both wet and dry are used. Suggested foods: mushrooms, cauliflower, protein gluten, eggplant slices.

Dry Batter

1 cup whole wheat flour
1 tbsp. garlic powder
1/4 cup nutritional yeast
1/2 tsp. paprika
1/2 tbsp. vege salt

1. Sift flour and add all other dry ingredients. Mix well.
2. Cover food pieces completely with batter and place in skillet with desired oil (hot). Cook until done on all sides.

Wet Batter

1 cup whole wheat flour
1/2 tsp. paprika
1/2 tsp. salt
1 1/2 cups water
1 tsp. garlic powder
1/4 cup tamari

Mix dry ingredients well and add water. Use more water or less for desired consistency.

When using the wet and dry batters together, begin with the wet batter. Completely immerse food pieces into wet batter and then completely cover wet pieces with the dry batter.

Place food pieces in skillet and cook as in dry batter recipe.

SAUCES AND GRAVIES

SOY BUTTER

TARTAR SAUCE

CREAMY SOY SAUCE

HOT SAUCE

GREEN PEA MUSHROOM SAUCE

BAR-B-QUE SAUCE

SWEET AND SOUR SAUCE

NUTRITIONAL YEAST GRAVY

TOMATO HONEY SAUCE

VEGETABLE GRAVY

SOY BUTTER

1 1/2 cups soy milk (see recipe, pg. 96)
juice of 1/2 lemon (strained)
2 1/2 cups oil

1. Place milk in blender. Start blending on medium speed. As milk blends, a hole will form in the center.
2. Pour oil slowly into hole until hole closes. Turn blender to high speed and add lemon juice. Turn off blender. Add more oil if needed. The hole in the center should be completely closed.
3. Stir well. Mixture should be stiff.

Season according to recipe. Use in cream pies, on sandwiches and when recipes call for Soy Butter.

Yields: 3 Cups

TARTAR SAUCE

1 1/2 cups soy butter
   (see recipe above)
3 tbsp. apple cider vinegar
1 cup pickle relish
   (see recipe, pg. 77)
2 tbsp. honey
pinch of salt

1. Blend all ingredients except relish.
2. Remove from blender and add relish.

Yields: 2 1/2 Cups

Sauces and Gravies

CREAMY SOY SAUCE

2 cups soy milk (see recipe, pg. 96)
1/2 tsp. salt

4-5 tbsp. nutritional yeast
1/2 cup soy margarine

1. Combine soy milk, nutritional yeast and salt. Stir until smooth.
2. Add soy margarine and stir constantly until smooth and thick.
This can be substituted for a basic white sauce.

Yields: 2 Cups

HOT SAUCE

8 oz. can tomato paste
3 tbsp. brown sugar or honey
4 tbsp. apple cider vinegar
2/3 cup grated garlic
2 tsp. oil
1 tsp. basil
1 level tsp. salt
4 oz. water

1. Mix all ingredients well.
2. Add water to desired consistency.

Yields: 2 Cups

GREEN PEA MUSHROOM SAUCE

1 lb. dried green peas (soaked overnight)
2 lbs. mushrooms (sliced)
1 stick margarine
salt (to taste)

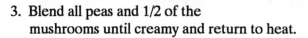

1. Boil peas until soft.
2. Saute mushrooms.
3. Blend all peas and 1/2 of the mushrooms until creamy and return to heat.
4. Add rest of saut ed mushrooms, margarine and salt.
5. Serve sauce over noodles or rice.

Yields: 2 Cups

BAR-B-QUE SAUCE

1/4 stick margarine   *12 oz. can tomato paste*
3 tbsp. molasses   *4 tbsp. honey*
1 1/2 tsp. apple cider vinegar *2 tbsp. garlic powder*
1 cup water   *salt (to taste)*
1 bay leaf
OPTIONAL: 1/8 cup tamari sauce

1. Place all ingredients in large sauce pan.
2. Simmer over low heat for 20 minutes.

Use over protein glutens, spaghetti or your favorite main dish.

Yields: 2 Cups

Sauces and Gravies

SWEET AND SOUR SAUCE

1 cup apple cider vinegar

1 medium orange (juiced)

1 medium beet, juiced or finely grated (**Add 1/4 cup water and let sit, then strain after 10 minutes**)

1/2 lb. brown sugar

1/4 tsp. powdered ginger or 1/8 tsp. fresh ground ginger

1/4 tbsp. grated nutmeg

4 tbs. cornstarch

1/2 cup water

1. Simmer all ingredients except 1/2 water in sauce pan over medium flame for 5 minutes.

2. Add remaining water to cornstarch to form a paste, stirring constantly.

3. Cook until thickened to desired consistency.

Serve over spring rolls, shish kabob, browned spiced protein gluten slices or use to make sweet and sour vegetables.

Yields: 2 Cups

NUTRITIONAL YEAST GRAVY

2-3 cups water for desired looseness/ thickness

1/4 cup whole wheat flour

salt (to taste)

1/4 cup oil

1/4 cup nutritional yeast

1/2 cup onions (diced medium)

1/2 cup bell pepper (diced medium)

1. Saute onions and peppers in oil; add flour and nutritional yeast.

2. Let brown a little, then add salt (to taste) and water. Stir. Let cook until thickened.

Yields: 3 1/2 Cups

TOMATO HONEY SAUCE

1 cup water	*1 tbsp. tomato paste*
1/2 tsp. salt	*1/4 cup honey*

1. Mix all ingredients in large skillet.
2. Cook until thickened.
3. Pour over favorite loaf after baking. Return loaf to oven until sauce is browned slightly.
   Yields: 2 Cups

VEGETABLE GRAVY

2 stalks celery	*1 large squash*
1/2 lb. stringbeans	*3 medium carrots*
1/2 stick margarine	*5 cloves garlic*
2 cups water	*3 tbsp. garlic powder*
2 tbsp. salt	*3 tbsp. corn starch*
OPTIONAL: 1/2 cup tamari sauce	

1. Dice all vegetables finely and put into a large saucepan with a small amount of water.
2. Steam, add garlic powder, paprika, tamari sauce and 2 tbsp. of salt. Stir well.
3. In a small bowl, mix corn starch and 1/2 cup water to make a paste. Add to vegetable mixture, stirring until thickened. Let simmer a few minutes. Remove from heat and add chopped garlic cloves.
4. Let stand, covered. Serve over rice, mashed potatoes or macaroni.
   Yields: 4 Servings

"And the Lord God planted a garden eastward in Eden; and there he put the man whom he had formed."

And out of the ground made the Lord God to grow every tree that is pleasant to the sight, and good for food; the tree of life also in the midst of the garden, and the tree of knowledge of good and evil."

Genesis 2: 8-9

SOUPS

POTATO-LEEK SOUP

POOR MAN'S SOUP

CREAM OF CELERY SOUP

BROWN LENTIL SOUP

ORANGE LENTIL SOUP

POTATO SOUP

BROCCOLI SOUP

VEGETABLE CHILI

GROUND NUT SOUP

Soul Vegetarian Cookbook

POTATO-LEEK SOUP

2 large leeks or onions (chopped)   3 large potatoes (chopped)
2 cups soy milk (see recipe, pg. 96)   3-4 cloves garlic
1/4 cup oil   vege salt (to taste)

1. Saute leeks in oil for 10 minutes.

2. Add sauteed leeks and potatoes to pot with enough hot water to cover.

3. Simmer until well cooked about 30 minutes.

4. Add milk. Cook until thick.

5. Season with vege salt and garlic. Serve hot or cold.

*Cold potato soup with lots of thinly sliced cucumbers is a good summer treat.

Yields: 2 Servings

POOR MAN'S SOUP

1/2 lb. tomatoes (sliced)   2 small eggplants (sliced)
2 medium onions (sliced)   1/2 head cauliflower (sliced)
1 medium bell pepper (sliced)   1 tsp. paprika
8 oz. bag noodles   4 oz. tomato paste
1 stick margarine   2 tbsp. nutritional yeast
1 tbsp. garlic powder   1 tbsp. salt
1 cup water   1 stalk broccoli
3 ears corn

1. In a large skillet, saute tomatoes, eggplant, onions, peppers and margarine.

2. In a medium pot, mix sauteed vegetables, water, tomato paste, garlic powder and paprika.

3. When soup comes to a boil, add noodles, salt and nutritional yeast, then turn down heat and let cook until noodles are al dente.

Yields: 8-9 Servings

Soups

CREAM OF CELERY SOUP

3 cups celery (chopped) *3/4 cup onions (diced)*
3 tbsp. whole wheat flour *3 tbsp. margarine*
4 cups soy milk (see recipe, pg. 96) *1 tsp. salt*
2 cups water *1 tbsp. parsley*

1. In a medium pot, combine celery, onions and water. Cook for 12-15 minutes or until tender.
2. In a large skillet, melt margarine and blend in flour and seasonings. Add milk and cook, stirring sauce until mixture thickens.
3. Add sauce to vegetable pot, cover and cook for 10 minutes more. Stir occasionally until soup thickens.
4. Garnish with parsley.
Yields: 6 Servings

BROWN LENTIL SOUP

3 cups brown lentil beans
1 package onion soup mix
3 celery stalks (diced)
1 stick margarine
2 tbsp. garlic powder
1 small onion
2 cloves garlic
5 cups water
1/2 cup soy sauce

1. Soak lentil beans overnight, then cook until soft.
2. Add vegetables. Cook until tender.
3. Add remaining ingredients. Simmer until done.
Yields: 8 Servings

ORANGE LENTIL SOUP

5 cups orange lentil beans
1 tbsp. salt
2 large carrots, diced
1 stick margarine
1 tbsp. garlic powder

1 large onion
5 stalks celery
1 potato, diced
1 tbsp. paprika

1. Cook orange lentils until creamy.
2. Add vegetables. Stir and cook for 20 minutes.
3. Add remaining ingredients. Simmer until done.
Yields: 8 Servings

POTATO SOUP

8 medium size potatoes
1/2 cup nutritional yeast
3 cloves garlic
1/2 tbsp. basil
1 1/2 sticks margarine
1/2 cup soy milk
   (see recipe, pg. 96)
1 tbsp. salt
1 quart water

1. Wash and dice potatoes. Cook in a medium size pot until almost done.
2. Add all other ingredients.
3. Simmer until done.
Yields: 8 Servings

Soups

BROCCOLI SOUP

10 broccoli heads	1 cup nutritional yeast
5 stalks celery (diced)	2 tbsp. garlic powder
2 tbsp. thyme	2 tbsp. salt
3 medium potatoes	2 tbsp. onion powder
1 stick margarine	4 quarts water

1. Cut broccoli flowers from stems and peel stems.
2. Grate stems and potatoes in food processor.
3. Cook in 4 quarts of water. When soup comes to boil, add all other ingredients.
4. Cook until done.

   Yields: 8 servings

VEGETABLE CHILI

2 lbs. red beans (picked and soaked)	4 tbsp. molasses
1 bulb garlic (diced)	2 tbsp. cumin (heaping)
2 tbsp. chili powder (heaping)	1 cup tamari
2 large onions	3 stalks celery
2 large green peppers	3 tbsp. brown sugar
1 cup mushrooms	1 cup tomato paste

1. Cook beans with molasses, cumin, brown sugar, chilli powder, tamari and tomato paste until beans are done.
2. Saute celery, onions and peppers.
3. Add vegetables to chili.
4. Simmer on medium heat for 10 minutes.
5. Add fresh garlic and mushrooms while chili is simmering.

   Yields: 10 Servings

GROUND NUT SOUP

8 cups water	1/4 lb. red cabbage
1/2 lb. green cabbage	1 ear yellow corn
3 medium zucchini squash	3 medium onions
1/2 lb. mushrooms	3 medium tomatoes
1/2 lb. okra	1 small can tomato paste
1 1/4 cups tamari	1 tbsp. salt
1 lb. natural smooth peanut butter	1 small eggplant

1. Mix peanut butter with enough water to dissolve the peanut butter to a smooth or loose consistency.
2. Put mixture into a large pot and let the peanut butter cook on low heat for thirty (30) minutes or until you see the oil separating from the peanut butter. *(Peanut butter may begin to stick to bottom of pot; be careful not to burn.)*
3. Add the remainder of water and allow the peanut butter and water to come to a boil.
4. Add the tomato paste to the mixture and let boil for 10 minutes.
5. Add the eggplant, corn, cabbage, onions, okra, mushrooms, tomatoes and zucchini squash.
6. Let soup cook until the vegetables get tender; then add salt and tamari for seasoning. *(Be careful not to make too salty.)* Soup will thicken as it cools.

Yields: 10-12 Servings

"When thou shalt besiege a city a long time, in making war against it to take it, thou shalt not destroy the trees thereof by forcing an axe against them; for thou mayest eat of them, and thou shalt not cut them down (for the tree of the field is man's life) to employ them in siege."

Deuteronomy 20:19

MAIN DISHES

PROTEIN (GLUTEN) DISHES

Raw Gluten   East Coast Protein Roast
Down South Bar-B-Que Twists   Nubian Nuggets (Mock Chicken)
Garvey Loaf   Garvey Burgers

GRAIN DISHES

Negev Bulgar (Cracked Wheat) Patties
Hebrew Rice
Jollouf Rice (Ghana's Most Popular Dish)
Fluffy Millet
Northeast African Hi-Protein Millet Patties
Amirah's Alabama (Spooned) Cornbread-Vegetable Dressing

PASTA DISHES

Lasagna
Macaroni & Cheese

VEGETABLE DISHES

Down-Home Greens
Beet Loaf
Picnic Potato Salad
Cheesy Potatoes
Cauliflower-In-A-Basket
Eggplant Parmesan
Stuffed Eggplant
Kermona's Pot Pie

TOFU DISHES

Battered Tofu
Scrambled Tofu
Tofulafels

LEGUME DISHES

Handburgers (Lentil Patties)
Stuffed Bell Peppers
Chickpea Loaf
Chickpea Patties
Watchi *(Ghanian Blackeyed Peas and Rice)*
Boss Baked Beans
Vegetable Chili Ole
Simple Middle-East Tacos

Soul Vegetarian Cookbook

RAW GLUTEN

2 lbs. whole wheat flour   *1 qt. water*

1. Mix whole wheat flour with water into a firm texture. Make sure all flour is mixed well (medium to firm dough).
2. Let set for 45 minutes (no less).
3. Put dough in a colander and while running cold water, continually squeeze dough to wash out starch from mixture. Continue to squeeze dough while at the same time making sure dough stays firmly together.
4. Keep rinsing until all graininess is removed and water is clear from rinsing.
5. Cover with water until ready to use.
   Yields: 1 lb.   *Gluten Uses: See Following Recipes.*

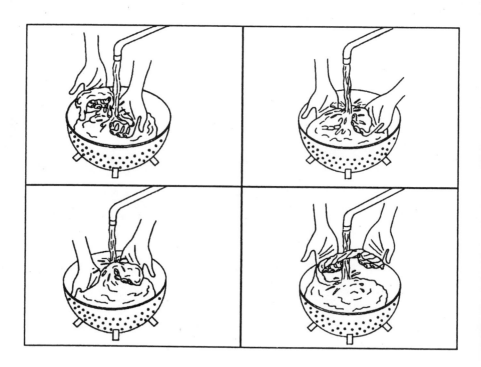

Main Dishes

EAST COAST PROTEIN ROAST

5 lbs. raw gluten
1 large onion (diced fine)
2 tbsp. sweet basil
2 tbsp. marjoram
1 1/2 tbsp. tamari sauce
1 sweet pepper (diced fine)
3 tbsp. nutritional yeast

2 tbsp. garlic powder
1 celery stalk (diced fine)
2 tbsp. paprika
2 cups water for basting
1 1/4 cups oil
salt (to taste)

1. Place raw gluten in a mixing bowl. Mix, pull and stretch gluten with seasonings and ingredients to evenly distribute.
2. Add 1/2 cup oil, tamari and yeast. Continue to pull and stretch.
3. Form seasoned gluten into loaf and place in roasting pan. Add water and rest of oil to pan and cover.
4. Bake in roasting pan at 375 degrees for 45 minutes. It will baste itself as it becomes brown.
5. Slice and serve with gravy or your favorite sauce.

Yields: 12 Servings

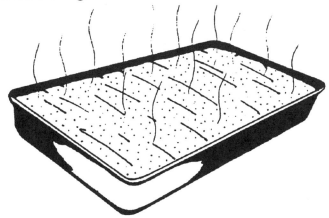

DOWN SOUTH BAR-B-QUE TWISTS

2 lbs. raw gluten
1/3 cup nutritional yeast
1 cup bar-b-que sauce (see recipe, pg. 18)
1/2 cup of peanut butter or tahini (sesame seed paste)
2 tbsp. paprika
2 tbsp. garlic powder
1 large onion (chopped fine)
1/2 cup hot oil

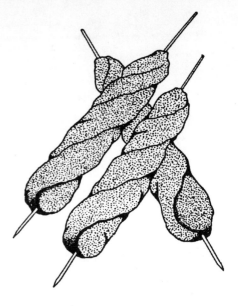

1. In a large bowl, add peanut butter, yeast, garlic powder and paprika to raw gluten. Mix well by pulling and stretching.
2. Saute onions in oil. Add onions and hot oil to seasoned gluten. (Hot oil breaks the gluten down and helps seasonings to penetrate.)
3. Continue to mix gluten well by pulling and stretching until consistency is stringy but doesn't tear apart.
4. Pull off small pieces of gluten and stretch and twist pieces into shapes similar to 6-8 inch bread sticks.
5. Place twists on lightly oiled cookie sheet and bake at 350 degrees for 1/2 hour or until crispy and brown on bottom. Brush twists with bar-b-que sauce and bake 10 minutes longer.

Yields: 12 Twists

Main Dishes

NUBIAN NUGGETS (Mock Chicken)

1 lb. raw gluten
2 cups nutritional yeast
4 tbsp. thyme
2 tbsp. curry powder
1/8 cup bar-b-que sauce (see recipe, pg. 18)

2 qts. water
1/4 cup salt
2 tbsp. garlic powder

1. Add all ingredients except gluten to water and bring to a boil.
2. Cut gluten into 4-6 inch pieces. Form pieces into small balls and drop into boiling water.
3. Stir occasionally until water comes to a second boil. Do not cover. Cook for 1 hour on medium heat.
4. Remove from heat and allow to cool.
5. Remove gluten from water and cut about 1/2 inch thick slices like steaks. Dry batter in seasoned flour or cornmeal and brown in lightly oiled skillet.
   Serve with bar-b-que sauce.

Yields: 8-10 Servings

GARVEY LOAF

5 cups raw gluten, boiled, then ground
1/2 cup whole wheat flour
2 tbsp. paprika
1/8 cup oil
1 small bell pepper (chopped fine)
2 packages onion soup mix
2 tbsp. garlic powder
1 tbsp. onion powder
2 tbsp. tamari sauce

1. Add all ingredients to ground gluten and mix well.
2. Shape into a loaf. Bake in loaf pan at 350 degrees for 1-1/2 hours.
3. During last 15 minutes, cover loaf with tomato-honey sauce, BBQ sauce, vegetable gravy or nutritional yeast gravy.
   Yields: 10 Servings

GARVEY BURGERS

1. Follow recipe for Garvey Loaf.
2. Shape into patties. Cook patties on both sides until browned in lightly oiled skillet.
   Yields: 12 Servings

Main Dishes

NEGEV BULGAR (CRACKED WHEAT) PATTIES

1/2 lb. bulgar
3 tbsp. onions (chopped fine)
4 tbsp. whole wheat flour (level)
1/3 cup oil
1 1/2 tbsp. ground sage

3 tbsp. peppers (chopped fine)
1/2 bulb garlic (chopped fine)
2 tbsp. paprika
1 1/2 tbsp. tamari

1. Pre-cook bulgar in pot with just enough water to cover until all water is absorbed. Cool.

2. Add sage, chopped vegetables, paprika, tamari and flour to cooked bulgar. Mix well.

3. Shape into patties and saute in oil on both sides until browned.

   Yields: 4 Servings

HEBREW RICE

1 medium bell pepper (chopped medium)
2 large cloves garlic (minced)
1 cup fresh mushrooms (sliced thinly)
2 medium onions (chopped medium)
OPTIONAL: Scrambled tofu (see recipe, pg. 48)

tamari sauce (to taste)
3 cups cooked browned rice
1/4 cup vegetable oil
1/4 cup celery (chopped)

1. Saute vegetables in oil in large skillet or saucepan.

2. Slowly add rice to vegetables and mix thoroughly.

3. Add garlic and tamari *(to taste)*.

4. Scrambled tofu can be added if desired.
   Yields: 4 Servings

JOLLOUF RICE
(GHANA'S MOST POPULAR DISH)

1 1/2 lbs. fresh tomatoes (sliced thin)
1 cup shredded cabbage
1 cup fresh spring peas
2 1/2 cups tomato paste
1/4 cup tamari
1 cup string beans
  (cut into bite-sized pieces)

2 1/4 lbs. rice
1 cup diced carrots
3 large onions
10 oz. palm oil*
3 cups water
salt (to taste)

1. Heat palm oil in skillet. Saute onions until light brown.
2. Gradually stir in tomato paste and cook.
3. Add 1/4 cup water and 1 tsp. salt.
5. Stir in vegetables; allow to steam.
6. Add rice and remaining water and salt; stir twice while cooking.
7. Allow to steam, reduce heat and simmer until done.

*Vegetable oil can be used if palm oil is not available.
Serve with salad, greens or any desired vegetable.
Yields: 20-25 Servings

Africans Love Large Gatherings!

Main Dishes

FLUFFY MILLET

1 cup millet *1 qt. water*
1 tsp. salt *1/4 stick margarine*

1. Put all ingredients except margarine in medium pan and boil for five minutes.
2. Turn down heat and simmer for 40 minutes. Turn off heat. Let steam, add margarine before serving.

   NOTE: Millet is one of seven grass seeds that are high in iron and protein. It contains no starch and is nutritional as well as delicious; rich in calcium!

   Delicious topped with grilled tomatoes and onions, or your favorite gravy. Makes a great base for meatless dishes.

Yields: 2 Servings

NORTHEAST AFRICAN HI-PROTEIN MILLET PATTIES

3 cups millet (cooked)
1/2 cup nut butter (cashew, almond, peanut, etc.)
1 tbsp. oil
2 tbsp. onion powder
1 tsp. salt
celery seed, rosemary, thyme (to taste)
OPTIONAL: 1 tbsp. tamari sauce

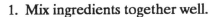

1. Mix ingredients together well.
2. Form into patties and brown on both sides in lightly oiled skillet. Serve with your favorite gravy.

Yields: 10 Servings

AMIRAH'S ALABAMA (SPOONED) CORNBREAD-VEGETABLE DRESSING

1 1/2 cups cornmeal	1 cup whole wheat flour
3 tbsp. oil	1 1/4 cups water
1 cup day-old bread (crumbled)	1 cup onions (diced fine)
1 cup bell peppers (diced fine)	1 cup celery (diced fine)
1/3 cup ground sage	1 cup carrots (diced fine)
1/2 cup stringbeans (diced fine)	1/2 cup squash (diced fine)
1/3 cup nutritional yeast	1 stick margarine
salt (to taste)	1/3 cup ground sage

1. Combine cornmeal and flour in mixing bowl. Add oil and water; mix well.
2. Bake at 350 degrees in an oiled baking pan until browned on top and bottom. Set aside and cool.
3. Put all diced vegetables in a steamer or a large sauce pan with 1 1/2 cups water. Steam until vegetables are done. Add magarine, sage, nutritional yeast and vege salt.

4. Crumble cornbread and bread crumbs together. Combine with vegetables and juice from vegetables in mixing bowl.
5. Place mixture in baking pan and bake for 30 minutes at 350 degrees.

TIP: *Steam vegetables in a steamer to preserve iron and vitamins.*

Yields: 4-6 Servings

Main Dishes

LASAGNA

1 package lasagna strips	*1 3/4 cups oil*
1 1/2 cups nutritional yeast	*1 tbsp. paprika*
1 tbsp. garlic powder	*2 lbs. gluten (boiled & ground)*
salt (to taste)	*1 cup water*
2 tbsp. nutritional yeast	*1 tbsp. carraway seeds*
3 tbsp. vege salt	*1 cup tomato paste*
2 tbsp. basil	

1. Boil lasagna strips al dente. (See Helpful Hints section)

2. Scramble crumbled gluten in skillet without oil with 1 tbsp. vege salt, 1 tbsp. carraway, 1 tbsp. basil and 2 tbsp. oil.

3. Make sauce by mixing 1 cup tomato paste, 1 cup water, 1 tbsp. basil, 2 tbsp. oil, 2 tbsp. vege salt, 2 tbsp. nutritional yeast. Bring to boil.

4. Make cheese. In blender mix 3 cups milk, 1/4 cup nutritional yeast, 1 tbsp. paprika, 1 tbsp. garlic powder and salt to taste. Slowly pour 1 1/2 cups oil until cheese is thickened.

5. Layout lasagna strips in baking pan. Spread scrambled gluten over strips. Spread cheese over gluten then spread tomato sauce. Continue layering in this manner until all ingredients are used.

6. Top with remaining tomato sauce and bake for 20 minutes at 350 degrees.

Yields: 8 Servings

MACARONI AND CHEESE

14 oz. macaroni noodles
4 cups water
1 tbsp. tumeric
1 cup soy milk (see recipe, pg. 96)
salt (to taste)

8 oz. or 1/2 block of tofu
1/2 cup tahini
5 tbsp. nutritional yeast
2 tbsp. margarine

1. Boil water in medium sauce pan and add noodles. Cut off heat. Let stand in hot water until al dente (5 minutes). Drain in colander. Run cold water over noodles to stop cooking process.

2. Blend tofu and milk in blender until smooth. Pour into mixing bowl. Add tahini, nutritional yeast, tumeric and salt to taste. Mix until smooth.

3. Add noodles to cheese mixture. Mix well.

4. Place in lightly oiled casserole dish, top with pats of margarine. Bake at 350 degrees for 20 minutes. Allow to cool before slicing.

Yields: 8-10 servings

DOWN-HOME GREENS

1 bunch collards (or other greens)
2 medium onions (cut in rings)
1 medium eggplant (chopped fine)
2 tbsp. garlic (chopped fine)
1 cup water
2 medium tomatoes (sliced)
1/2 cup oil
salt (to taste)

Yields: 4-6 Servings

1. Shred greens.

2. Cook in large skillet or medium pot in 1/2 cup oil and 1 cup water or in pressure cooker with eggplant for 12 minutes.

3. Saute onions with tomatoes. Add garlic and salt to taste. Stir into greens in skillet after pouring off pot liquor.

Main Dishes

BEET LOAF

1 large carrot
1 tbsp. celery (chopped fine)
1 tbsp. onions (chopped fine)
1 clove garlic (minced)
2 tbsp. whole wheat flour
1 tbsp. paprika

1 medium beet
1 tbsp. peppers (chopped fine)
1/2 cup oil
1/3 cup cornmeal (sifted)
1/2 tbsp. tamari sauce

1. Grate beet and carrot on fine side of grater. Mix thoroughly with other ingredients.
2. Shape into loaf and place into an oiled 9" pan. Bake at 350 degrees for 45 minutes. Loaf can be covered with sauce or gravy.

(Potatoes can be substituted for beets)

Yields: 5 Servings

PICNIC POTATO SALAD

7 medium potatoes (steamed and diced medium)
1 medium onion (diced finely)
1 small red pepper (diced finely)
1 small green pepper (diced finely)
2/3 cup celery (diced finely)
1/2 cup pickle relish with juice
(see recipe, pg. 77)
1 tbsp. salt
1 tbsp. tumeric
1 1/2 cups soy butter
(see recipe, pg. 16)
1/2 tbsp. mustard
1/3 cup nutritional yeast

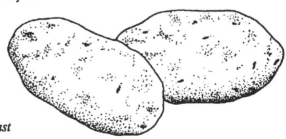

1. Mix all ingredients well. Serve chilled.

Yields: 8 Servings

Soul Vegetarian Cookbook

CHEESY POTATOES

2 lbs. white potatoes (sliced)   *1 large onion (sliced)*
2 cups soy cheese   *1/4 cup parsley (chopped fine)*
1 tsp. salt   *1 tbsp. paprika*

1. Wash and steam potatoes al dente. Do not overcook.

2. In a large baking pan, alternate layers of sliced potatoes, onions and soy cheese. Top with remaining layer of cheese.

3. Sprinkle paprika and parsley on top.

4. Bake at 350 degrees for 30 minutes or until cheese is brown.

Yields: 4-5 Servings

CAULIFLOWER-IN-A-BASKET

1 medium head cauliflower   *1 lb. whole wheat flour*
1/2 tbsp. paprika   *3/4 tbsp. garlic powder*
1 tbsp. salt   *1/3 cup oil*
2/3 cup water   *tamari sauce (to taste)*

1. Clean and separate cauliflower into individual bite-sized pieces.

2. Sift flour and add garlic powder, paprika and salt. Mix well.

3. Take 1/3 of flour batter, mix with tamari sauce, water and 3/4 tbsp. of oil and stir into a creamy paste.

4. Place pieces of cauliflower in wet batter, then into dry batter.

5. Brown in skillet on medium flame in remaining oil.

6. Brown slowly on all sides until tender.

7. Other vegetables like mushrooms, carrots, broccoli, etc. can be battered in this manner.
   Yields: 3-4 Servings

Main Dishes

EGGPLANT PARMESAN

3 medium eggplants
4 cups soy cheese
(see recipe, pg. 73)
1/4 cup lemon juice
whole wheat batter, wet and dry (see recipes pg. 13)
3 tbsp. corn meal
2 large onions (thinly sliced)
12 oz. can tomato paste
1/4 cup oil
1 tbsp. blackstrap molasses
1/4 tsp. brown sugar

1. Add cornmeal to dry batter.
2. Slice eggplant lengthwise into thin slices.
3. Dip eggplant slices into wet batter, then into dry batter.
4. Brown battered slices in skillet in 1/8 cup oil.
5. Make sauce using tomato paste, molasses, brown sugar and lemon juice.
6. In ungreased oven pan, layer sauce, battered eggplant slices, thinly sliced onions, soy cheese. Layer in this manner until all ingredients have been used, allowing cheese to be last layer.
7. Bake at 350 degrees for approximately 20 minutes or until parmesan is firm.

Yields: 6 Servings

Soul Vegetarian Cookbook

STUFFED EGGPLANT

2 tbsp. fresh parsley (chopped fine)	2 tbsp. tamari sauce
2 small peppers (chopped fine)	1 1/2 tbsp. garlic powder
2 small onions (chopped fine)	1/4 cup brown rice
2 small stalks celery (chopped fine)	1 tbsp. paprika
1 small tomato (diced medium)	2 medium eggplants

1. Cut eggplant in half. Then scoop out the inside of the eggplant with a spoon. Break up with a fork.

2. Pre-cook eggplant shells in 1 cup of boiling water for 5 minutes.

3. Cook rice with 1/2 cup of water.

4. Mix eggplant, pepper, onion, celery and tomato well. Add rice, paprika, garlic powder, tamari and parsley. Continue to mix well.

5. Stuff each eggplant shell with filling and bake at 350 degrees for 1/2 hour.

Yields: 4 Servings

KERMONA'S POT PIE

STEP 1 - FILLING

1 lb. potatoes (diced medium or fine)

1/8 lb. carrots (diced medium or fine)

1/2 stalk celery (diced medium or fine)

1/8 lb. bell peppers (diced medium or fine)

1 lb. onions (diced medium or fine)

1 8 oz. package dried vegetables

1 lb. stringbeans (optional)

1/2 cup oil

1/2 tsp. salt

1. Saute half the amount of onions, peppers and all the dried vegetables.

2. Stir vegetables and salt. Add nutritional yeast gravy to vegetable mixture.

Main Dishes

STEP 2 - GRAVY
See Nutritional Yeast Gravy in SAUCES AND GRAVY.
*Saute remaining onions and peppers for gravy mixture.

STEP 3 - CRUST
2 lbs. flour	1/4 cup oil
2 sticks margarine	1/2 cup water

1. Rub margarine and flour together until it reaches the texture of coarse cornmeal. Add in oil, and 1/2 cup water. Mix well until soft dough is formed.
2. Roll out dough, fit into shape of baking pan. Use rest of dough for top crust.
3. Pour mixture into crust.
4. Add top crust. Prick crust with fork to vent steam.
5. Bake pie at 350 degrees until crust is browned on top and bottom.

Yields: 10-12 Servings

Soul Vegetarian Cookbook

BATTERED TOFU

1 16oz. block tofu (sliced 5 times)	1/3 cup water
2 tbsp. tamari sauce	1/4 cup oil

BATTER

1 cup cornmeal	1/4 cup flour
1 tsp. salt	1/3 cup nutritional yeast
3 tbsp. garlic powder	2 tbsp. paprika

1. Combine water and tamari sauce together.
2. Put slices in tamari sauce to marinate. Set aside.
3. Mix dry batter ingredients and batter slices.
4. Brown tofu on both sides on grill or in skillet.

Yields: 2 Servings

SCRAMBLED TOFU

1 16oz. block tofu	2 tbsp. peppers (chopped fine)
2 tbsp. onions (chopped fine)	2 tbsp. nutritional yeast
tamari sauce (to taste)	1/2 tsp. tumeric
1/2 stick margarine	1 tbsp. garlic powder

1. Melt margarine in skillet, saute onions and peppers.
2. Add tofu and mash with fork.
3. Add remaining ingredients and scramble until water from tofu is cooked out.

Additional spices can be added for your taste: Onion powder, parsley flakes, basil.

Yields: 2 Servings

TIP: *Tofu is available at health food stores and some supermarkets.*

Main Dishes

TOFULAFELS

1 cup celery & peppers (chopped/sautéed) *1 lb. tofu*
1 tbsp. garlic powder *1/3 tsp. sweet basil*
1 tbsp. apple cider vinegar *3 oz. wheatgerm*
1 tbsp. flour *dry batter (see recipe pg. 13)*
2 tbsp. coriander *1 tsp. cumin*
1/2 tsp. salt *1 1/2 tbsp. oil*
1/2 cup onions (chopped fine)

1. Mix all ingredients well, except batter. Shape into one inch balls.
2. Roll each ball in dry batter.
3. Brown balls in skillet with small amount of oil. If balls crumble, add water by spoonfuls until they hold.

Yields: 25 Balls

HANDBURGERS (LENTIL PATTIES)

1/2 lb. brown lentils (soaked) *1/8 cup water (to blend)*
1/4 cup onions (chopped fine) *1/4 cup celery (chopped fine)*
1/4 cup red peppers (chopped fine) *1 cup oil*
2 cloves garlic (minced) *1 tsp. paprika*
1/8 cup tamari sauce (optional) *salt (to taste)*

1. Process soaked lentils in food processor or blender, using fine chopper, along with onions, celery, peppers and garlic.
2. Add 1/8 cup water and 1/2 cup oil and spices as you process for a smooth but firm mix.
3. Drop by tablespoon into hot skillet, brown on both sides, using 2 tbsp. oil per skillet.

Yields: 10 Patties

Soul Vegetarian Cookbook

STUFFED BELL PEPPERS

1/2 lb. unseasoned/browned handburger mix

1 medium bell pepper (diced)

1 stick margarine

2 1/2 medium onions (diced)

1/2 lb. mushrooms (sliced)

1 1/2 tbsp. garlic powder

2 tbsp. tamari sauce

1/2 tbsp. salt

1 1/2 tbsp. honey

1 tbsp. oregano

1/2 tsp. thyme

2 cups cooked brown rice

12 oz. can tomato paste

9 medium bell peppers

2 tbsp. fresh garlic (crushed)

2 cups soy cheese (see recipe pg. 73)

1. Saute margarine, onions, peppers and mushrooms. Add garlic powder and tamari sauce. Cover and steam 5 minutes.

2. Mix browned handburger mix, rice and remaining ingredients to steamed vegetables.

3. Slice tops and core bell peppers. Steam for 10 minutes or until slightly tender.

4. Make sauce, mixing tomato paste, honey, oregano, thyme and fresh garlic. Bring to a boil, cover, let stand.

5. Stuff handburger mix into bell peppers, leaving room at the top for 1/2 tbsp. tomato sauce and 1/2 tbsp. soy cheese. Bake for 45 minutes at 325 degrees.

Yields: 9 Servings

Main Dishes

CHICK PEA LOAF

1 lb. cooked chick peas (soaked)	*1/3 cup celery (chopped fine)*
1/3 cup onions (chopped fine)	*1/3 cup oil*
1 tsp. salt	*2 tbsp. parsley (chopped fine)*
1/2 tbsp. tamari sauce (optional)	*1 tsp. dried sage (ground)*
1 tbsp. chick pea flour or	*1/4 cup tomato-honey sauce*
whole wheat flour	*(see recipe pg. 20)*

1. In grinder or food processor, add a small amount of water and grind chick peas; add ingredients to chickpeas and mix well.
2. Put into shallow, well-oiled baking dish.
3. Bake at 320 degrees for 40 minutes or until al dente.
4. Spread tomato-honey sauce on top and bake until brown.

Yields: 7 Servings

CHICK PEA PATTIES

2 cups chick peas (soaked)	*1/2 cup onions*
1 cup oil	*1/2 cup peppers*
1/2 cup whole wheat flour	*1/2 cup corn meal*
1 tbsp. coriander	*salt (to taste)*

1. Grind chick peas in blender or food processor with just enough water to make mixture smooth.
2. Add vegetables and dry ingredients to chick peas.
3. Add 1/2 cup of oil and mix well then shape into patties.
4. Cook patties on each side in skillet with 2 tbsp. oil until golden brown.

Yields: 12 Servings

WATCHI
(Ghanian Blackeyed Peas and Rice)

2 lbs. blackeyed peas (soaked over-night)   4 tbsp. oil
2 cups tomato paste   3 large onions (sliced)
1 cup vegetable oil   1/2 lb. rice
3 tbsp. whole wheat flour (heaping)   1 1/2 tbsp. nutmeg (level)
salt (to taste)

1. Cook peas with 4 tbsp. oil until almost done.
2. Add salt to taste.
3. Add rice to blackeyed peas.
4. Allow to steam.
5. Reduce heat, simmer until done.

SAUCE
1. Heat 8 oz. oil in skillet.
2. Add flour, stir until brown.
3. Add onions, cook until brown.
4. Add tomato paste and stir until well cooked.
5. Add water according to desired thickness. (IT SHOULD NOT BE SOUPY)
6. Add nutmeg, allow to cook.
7. Sauce is served over blackeyed peas and rice with salad, greens or any vegetable.

Yields: 20-25 Servings

Main Dishes

BOSS BAKED BEANS

1 lb. dried beans (soak 24 hours)
1 tbsp. paprika
2 tbsp. salt
2 tbsp. oil
1/4 cup raw sugar or 1/8 cup honey

1 tbsp. garlic powder
2 tbsp. molasses
1/2 tbsp. basil
1 cup tomato paste

1. Pressure beans for 30 minutes in water 3 inches over beans.
2. Put tomato paste in mixing bowl and add a cup water. Add sugar, oil and spices and mix well.
3. Bake in baking dish uncovered for 1/2 hour at 375 degrees. Let cool.

You can vary dish by using navy, soy, and other white beans.

Yields: 6 Servings

VEGETABLE CHILI OLE

2 lbs. red beans (soaked)
1 lb. fresh tomatoes (chopped)
2 cloves garlic (minced)
3 tbsp. cumin
8 oz. tomato paste
3 tbsp. brown sugar
1 16 oz. package spaghetti
2 large onions (diced medium)
3 stalks celery (diced medium)
2 large bell peppers (diced medium)
salt (to taste)

1. Simmer beans with tomatoes, cumin, brown sugar and salt.

2. Saute celery, onions, peppers in separate pan and add to chili.

3. Add tomato paste to thicken base; simmer for 10 minutes. Add fresh garlic while chili is simmering.

4. Serve over spaghetti.

Optional: Add browned, scrambled gluten bits as an extra treat.

Yields: 4 servings

Soul Vegetarian Cookbook

SIMPLE MIDDLE-EAST TACOS

1 package tortilla shells
2 cloves garlic (crushed)
3/4 tsp. ground coriander
1 cup shredded lettuce
1/2 cups soy cheese (see recipe pg. 73)
1 cup dried kidney beans (soaked 24 hours)

1/4 cup tahini
2 tbsp. lemon juice
1/2 tsp. cumin
1 cup tomatoes (diced)
1 cup onions (diced)

1. Pressure beans in water 3 inches over beans for 45 minutes. Pour off water.
2. Puree together beans, tehinah, garlic, lemon juice, cumin and coriander.
3. Let stand one-half hour at room temperature. Fill tortilla shells with mixture. Place sandwiches in hot oven for six minutes. Take out and layer with garnishes of lettuce, tomato, onions and soy cheese.

Yields: 8-10 servings

"And God said, Behold I have given you every herb bearing seed, which is upon the face of all the earth, and every tree, in which is the fruit of a tree yielding seed; to you it shall be for meat."

Genesis 1:29

"And the earth brought forth vegetation and herb yielding seed after its kind, and the tree yielding fruit, whose seed was in itself, after its kind; and God saw that it was good."

Genesis 1:12

RAW DISHES

SALADS - SIDE DISHES
Avocado Salad
Carrot Supreme Salad
Super "Live" Salad
Tomato, Cucumber and Sprout Salad
Marinated Pickled Beets
Parsley Salad
Stringbean Salad

MAIN DISHES
Raw Chopped Suey
Raw Vegetable Soup
Corn Salad
Marinated Tofu Salad
Tofu Salad
Swiss Chard Salad
Eggplant Salad
Raw Sweet Potato Salad

A LA CARTE
Strawberry Heaven
Fruit Salad Combo
Dried Fruit Candy

AVOCADO SALAD

1 medium avocado
1 tbsp. alfalfa sprouts
1 small tomato (diced)
2 tbsp. oil

1/3 lb. mushrooms (sliced)
1/3 tsp. salt
1/3 onion (chopped fine)

1. Cut avocado in half, remove seed and spoon avocado out of shell. Chop into medium sized cubes.
2. Add remaining ingredients and mix well.

Olive oil is suggested for this recipe.

Yields: 2 Servings

CARROT SUPREME SALAD

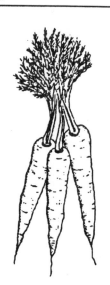

4 cups carrot pulp (from 2 lb. carrots juiced in electric juicer)
1/4 cup onions (chopped fine)
1/4 cup celery (chopped fine)
1/2 cup nutritional yeast
1/2 cup pickle relish (see recipe, pg. 77)
2 tbsp. olive oil
2 tbsp. honey (optional)
3/4 cup soy butter (see recipe, pg. 16)
1/2 cup carrot juice (drink the rest, very refreshing)
1/2 tbsp. vege salt

1. Mix all ingredients well.
2. Serve as sandwich, on toast or crackers, with celery, carrot sticks or on a bed of lettuce or bed of sprouts.

Yields: 4 Servings

Raw Dishes

SUPER "LIVE" SALAD

1 head romaine or bibb lettuce
2 medium tomatoes (sliced)
1/2 cup sliced mushrooms
1/4 cubed avocado
1 onion (chopped)

1/2 lb. spinach
1 cucumber (diced)
3 small carrots (grated)
5 radishes (grated)
1 clove garlic (minced)

1. Wash all ingredients well and drain off excess water.
2. Tear lettuce and spinach into small pieces. Place in a bowl.
3. Toss together with remaining ingredients.

Yields: 8 Servings

TOMATO, CUCUMBER AND SPROUT SALAD

1 cucumber (chopped fine)
1 tomato (chopped fine)
2 cloves garlic (chopped fine)
1/4 cup bean sprouts
1/4 cup onions (chopped)
2 tbsp. oil
vege salt (optional)

1. Wash and rinse vegetables. Mix cucumbers, tomato and onions together.
2. Add sprouts, oil and garlic. Mix well.
3. Add vegetable salt if desired.

Yields: 2 Servings

Soul Vegetarian Cookbook

MARINATED PICKLED BEETS

5 medium beets (steamed tender & sliced)   *1/3 cup apple cider vinegar*
1/3 cup honey   *1/4 cup olive oil*
1 clove garlic   *vege salt (to taste)*

1. Blend liquid mixture together including garlic.

2. Pour over beets which have been sliced.

3. Let stand at least one hour before serving.

Yields: 4 Servings

PARSLEY SALAD

1 bunch of parsley   *olive oil*
4 romaine lettuce leaves   *3 tomatoes*
1 tbsp. dill (fresh)   *salt (optional)*

Pull leaves of parsley off stems. Shred lettuce. Dice tomatoes. Cut dill small. (If you use iceberg lettuce, tear, do not cut). Add desired amount of olive oil. Mix throughly.

Yields: 1 Serving

STRING BEAN SALAD

1 small bell pepper (diced)   *1 medium onion (diced)*
2 medium pickles (diced)   *1 celery stalk (diced)*
3 tbsp. nutritional yeast   *1/2 tsp. garlic powder*
3/4 tsp. paprika   *salt (to taste)*
1 lb. young, tender baby   *Olive oil or your*
    string beans (chopped fine)   *favorite dressing*

Combine all vegetables. Add spices, toss well. Mix in desired amount of olive oil or your favorite dressing. BON APPETIT!

Yields: 2-4 Servings

Raw Dishes

RAW CHOPPED SUEY

3 heads of cauliflower flowers (sliced)
1-2 bell peppers (sliced thin)
1 1/2 cups sprouts
1 tbsp. garlic powder
3 heads of broccoli flowers (sliced)
1/2 block tofu (cubed)
1/2 lb. bulgar (soaked)
1/2 cup snow peas
3 stalks of celery (sliced in long thin strips)

1-2 onions (sliced thin)
1 carrot (grated on large side)
1/2 cup olive oil
1 tsp. paprika
3-4 tbsp. nutritional yeast
6 lg. mushrooms (thinly sliced)
tamari (to taste)
salt (to taste)

1. Pick, clean and presoak bulgar. Set aside for 3 hours. Season with paprika, salt and garlic powder.

2. Marinate vegetables in olive oil and tamari sauce for 3 hours. Add nutritional yeast to make gravy.

3. Before serving add sprouts for crispness and serve over portions of bulgar. *(Couscous can be subsituted for bulgar)*

Yields: 2 Servings

RAW VEGETABLE SOUP

2 medium tomatoes
1 small carrot
3-4 cloves garlic
2-3 tbsp. oil
salt (to taste)
1 tsp. paprika
1/2 tsp. basil

1/2 medium onion
1 small bell pepper
parsley sprigs
2 cups water
2 stalks celery
1-2 tbsp. nutritional yeast

1. Wash vegetables well. Cut into quarters for easy blending.

2. In blender, blend vegetables, spices, gradually adding water to smooth blending process.

3. At serving time, top with 1 tsp. nutritional yeast and a sprig or two of parsley.

Yields: 2-3 Servings

CORN SALAD

1/2 lb. corn
1/4 cup onions (chopped fine)
1/2 cup soy butter (see recipe, pg. 16)
salt (to taste)

1/4 cup peppers (chopped fine)
1/4 cup celery (chopped fine)
garlic (to taste)

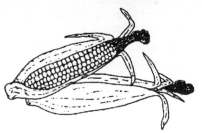

1. Wash all vegetables.
2. Cut corn off cob. Mix vegetables.
3. Add soy butter and mix ingredients well.

Yields: 2-3 Servings

MARINATED TOFU SALAD

1 block tofu (16 oz.)
1/2 cup olive oil
1/3 cup water
2 cups mushrooms (thinly sliced)

1 small onion (sliced thin)
1/4 cup tamari sauce
1/2 tsp. garlic powder
1/3 tsp. paprika

1. Cut tofu into cubes.
2. Add sliced onions and mushrooms to all other ingredients.
3. Toss well.
4. Marinate 1-2 hours or to desired taste.

Yields: 4 Servings

TIP: *The secret of this intensely flavored salad is the long marination; the actual preparation time is only 15 minutes.*

Raw Dishes

TOFU SALAD

8 oz. block tofu
2 tbsp. soy butter (recipe, pg. 16)
2 tbsp. pickle relish (optional)
1 small green pepper (chopped)
vege salt (to taste)

1 stalk celery (chopped)
1 scallion (chopped)
1 tbsp. honey
2 tbsp. nutritional yeast

1. Mash tofu and mix in other ingredients.
2. Can be served alone, on whole grain bread or in pita bread.

Yields: 4 Servings

SWISS CHARD SALAD

3 large leaves, young tender swiss chard
1 medium cucumber (diced)
2 tbsp. olive oil or favorite dressing
2 cloves fresh garlic (minced)

1 small tomato (diced)
1 tbsp. onions (diced)
1 medium avocado (sliced)
vege salt (to taste)

1. Shred swiss chard.
2. Mix in other ingredients except avocado.
3. Place salad in serving dish. Top with avocado slices and favorite dressing (or use olive oil).

Delicious with Nicamah's Creamy Butter Dressing (see Recipe pg 70).

Yields: 2 Servings

63

Soul Vegetarian Cookbook

EGGPLANT SALAD

1 medium eggplant (diced small)	*2 tbsp. onions (diced fine)*
2 tbsp. celery (diced fine)	*3/4 tsp. paprika*
3/4 tsp. vege salt (to taste)	*1 small pickle (diced fine)*
juice of (1) lemon (optional)	*2 tbsp. tamari sauce*
2 tbsp. nutritional yeast	*2 tbsp. bell pepper (diced fine)*
3/4 tsp. garlic powder	*pinch of parsley leaves*
2 cups water	*2 tbsp. olive oil or soy butter (see recipe, pg. 16)*

1. Marinate eggplant for one hour in plain water <u>or</u> lemon water <u>or</u> salt water, let stand to drain.

2. Squeeze water out of eggplant.

3. Add diced vegetables and season to taste.

4. Add olive oil or soy butter and mix well.

5. Place in refrigerator until ready to serve. Top with parsley and serve.

   Yields: 2-3 Servings

RAW SWEET POTATO SALAD

1/2 lb. sweet potatoes	*1/4 tsp. nutmeg*
1/2 cup brown sugar <u>or</u> 1/4 cup honey	*1 cup soy butter*
1/4 tsp. cinnamon	*1/2 cup raisins or coconut*

1. Grate sweet potatoes on fine side of grater.

2. Stir in sugar, soy butter, nutmeg and cinnamon.

3. Add raisins or coconut. Use enough soy butter to keep salad moist but not soggy.

4. Chill and serve. *Do not refrigerate for more than one day.*

   Yields: 2-4 Servings

Raw Dishes

STRAWBERRY HEAVEN

4 medium bananas
1/2 lb. strawberries
1 cup soy milk
1 tbsp. honey
1 1/3 cups oil
2 tbsp. coconut (heaping)
wheatgerm (optional)
chopped nuts (optional)

1. In blender, mix soy milk and honey. As you blend, slowly pour in 1 1/3 cups of oil until hole in center closes and soy butter is thick.
2. Add 1 banana and 10 medium strawberries. Chill mixture.
3. Dice remaining bananas and strawberries.
4. In a dessert dish, layer bananas, cream mix and strawberries until all ingredients are used.
5. Add a last layer of cream and top with any combination of coconut, nuts and wheatgerm and one strawberry in center.

This fruit recipe can be created with any combination of non-citrus fruit that is in season, excluding mango, peaches or pineapple.

Can be eaten as a breakfast or dessert.

FRUIT SALAD COMBO

2 lbs. peaches   1 1/2 lbs. bananas
2 pints strawberries   1/2 cup brown sugar or honey

1. Blend 1/2 pint of strawberries, 2 peaches and 1 banana with brown sugar or honey to make your sauce.
2. Chop remaining fruit; place in a mixing bowl. Add sauce. Mix well. Chill and serve.
   Yields: 7 Servings

Soul Vegetarian Cookbook

DRIED FRUIT CANDY

1/2 lb. organic raisins
1/2 lb. organic figs
1/4 lb. coconut

1/2 lb. organic dates
1/4 lb. walnuts (crushed)

1. Cut fruit into small pieces and mix well.
2. Add crushed nuts a little at a time.
3. Shape into balls and roll each ball into the coconut.

VARIATIONS

You may use any dried fruit such as prunes, apricots, etc. or you may use all of them. You do not have to cook or refrigerate.

Yields: 20 Balls

Raw Dishes

EASY SPROUTING

Sprouts are young shoots that emerge from seeds, beans and grains. During the sprouting process, starch is changed to simple sugar and maintains the **B-Complex** enabling the sugar to become quick energy.

Sprouting is one of the fastest ways of improving the nutritional value of foods. Almost any whole, natural seed will sprout. Broken seeds or beans **will not** sprout, neither will heat-treated seeds or beans.

The most popular for sprouting are:

Alfalfa ("King of sprouts")   *Lentils*

Mung Beans (Oriental cooking)   *Wheat Berries*

Best length growth:

1 - 2 inches   *1 1/2 - 2 1/2 inches*

1 inch   *1/4 inch*

A combination of radish seeds mixed with alfalfa and sprouted together is high in vitamin C and excellent for salads.

DIRECTIONS

Pick over (to get out rocks and broken seeds) and wash 1/4 cup of desired seed or grain; place in quart jar; cover with warm water and soak overnight (cover top of jar with cheese cloth and secure with a rubber-band). Drain off soaking water and rinse with room temperature water and drain again. Keep seeds moist but not wet. Turn jar on its side; keep in warm, dark place until sprouts appear, then place in sunlight. **IMPORTANT**: Rinse sprouts twice daily for 2 - 5 days, after which time they can be eaten or refrigerated and kept for 3 days at the most.

HAPPY SPROUTING!!!

SALAD DRESSINGS, DIPS AND RELISHES

King's Dressing

Nicamah's Creamy Butter Dressing

Hebrew Dressing

Thousand Island Dressing

Prince Dressing

Tomato Salad Dressing

Lemon & Garlic Dressing

Tofu Salad Dressing

Soy Cheese

Cottage Cheese

Tofu Rye Chesse

Tofu Garlic Cheese

Baht Ami's Dip

Parsley Dip

Sunflower Seed Spread

Cranberry -- Orange Relish

Pickles

Sweet Pickle Relish

Soul Vegetarian Cookbook

KING'S DRESSING

1/2 cup red wine vinegar　　　　*1 small onion*
3 tbsp. herb seasoning　　　　*tamari sauce (to taste)*
juice of 2 lemons　　　　*3 tbsp. honey*
3 tbsp. garlic powder

1. Place all ingredients in blender and blend until creamy.

Yields: 1 Cup

NICAMAH'S CREAMY
BUTTER DRESSING

1 cup soy milk　　　　*1 1/3 cups oil*
2 tbsp. apple cider vinegar　　　　*1/3 cup nutritional yeast*

1. In blender, blend soy milk, nutritional yeast and vinegar.

2. While blending a hole will appear in the middle of mixture. Slowly pour oil into the middle of hole until hole closes.

Yields: 2 Cups

HEBREW DRESSING

1 cup vegetable oil　　　　*1/4 cup apple cider vinegar*
4 tbsp. honey　　　　*1 tbsp. vege salt*
1 tsp. paprika　　　　*1 small onion*

1. Blend all ingredients in blender.

Yields: 1 1/2 Cups

Salad Dressings, Dips, and Relishes

THOUSAND ISLAND DRESSING

1/3 onion (chopped)
2 cups soy butter (see recipe pg. 16)
2 tbsp. green pepper (chopped fine)
1 cup pickle relish (see recipe pg. 77)
1 small tomato
1/2 stalk celery
3 tbsp. honey

1. Place onion, celery and tomato into blender.
2. Add soy butter to mixture and blend.
3. Add chopped green pepper and relish. Blend while adding honey until creamy.

Yields: 4 Cups

PRINCE DRESSING

1 1/2 cups oil
7 medium cloves garlic
2 1/2 cups nutritional yeast
2 1/2 cups water
1/4 cup tamari sauce

1. Blend oil, garlic and tamari together in blender.
2. Add nutritional yeast.
3. Pour water slowly to make dressing creamy. Add more water if necessary.

Yields: 3 Cups

TOMATO SALAD DRESSING

1/2 cup tomatoes
2 small onions (cubed)
1 1/2 cups oil
3 tbsp. water
1 tbsp. vege salt
1 tbsp. garlic powder
2 tbsp. honey
1 tbsp. pickle relish (see recipe, pg. 77)

1. Put just enough tomatoes and honey into blender, just enough to cover blades. Add water to liquify mixture.
2. Pour vegetable oil slowly in the middle of mixture until hole in the middle closes and dressing has slightly thickened.
3. Add remaining ingredients. If thicker dressing is desired, add more oil.

Yields: 3 Cups

LEMON AND GARLIC DRESSING

juice of two (2) lemons
1/4 cup tamari sauce
1/2 cup soy milk
2 tbsp. herb seasoning (your favorite brand)

2 cups vegetable oil
4 garlic cloves (crushed)

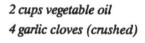

1. Blend milk, lemon, tamari and garlic together in blender.
2. Add oil and seasoning to center until hole closes.

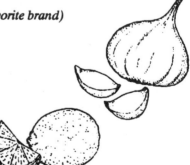

Yields: 3 Cups

Salad Dressings, Dips, and Relishes

TOFU SALAD DRESSING

1 1/2 lbs. tofu (drained)
1/3 cup safflower oil (or favorite oil)
1/2 tsp. basil
1/2 tsp. oregano
1/3 cup water

2 tbsp. tamari
2 tbsp. apple cider vinegar
1/2 tsp. garlic powder
1/2 tsp. onion powder

1. Puree all ingredients in blender until smooth and creamy.
   Yields: 2 Cups

SOY CHEESE

5 cups soy butter (see recipe, pg. 16)
1/4 tsp. garlic powder
1 tsp. paprika

7 tbsp. nutritional yeast
1/4 cup tamari sauce

1. Blend all ingredients together until a desired cheesy texture and taste is acquired.
2. Use in any recipes that call for soy cheese.
   Yields: 5 Cups

COTTAGE CHEESE

1/2 cup crumbled tofu
3 tsp. soy butter (see recipe, pg. 16)

pinch of salt

1. Place all ingredients in small bowl.
2. Mix well.
3. Place in mold if desired.
4. Serve with vegetable salad or fruit salad.
   Yields: 2 Servings

TOFU RYE CHEESE

1 1/2 lbs. crumbled tofu
1/2 cup nutritional yeast
1 1/2 cups soy butter (see recipe, pg. 16)
5 tbsp. ground rye
2 tbsp. paprika
salt (to taste)

1. In a bowl, blend all ingredients and serve.

   Yields: 2 1/2 Cups

TOFU GARLIC CHEESE

1 1/2 lbs. crumbled tofu
2 tbsp. garlic (steamed & crushed)
1 1/2 cups soy butter (see recipe, pg. 16)
salt (to taste)
1/2 cup nutritional yeast
3 tbsp. garlic powder
1 tsp. fresh garlic (grated)

1. In a medium bowl, mix tofu and all other ingredients well.
2. Serve on crackers or toast.

   Yields: 2 1/2 Cups

BAHT AMI'S DIP

3 cups soy butter (see recipe pg. 16)
juice of 1 large lemon
2 tbsp. garlic powder
1/2 lb. dried onion
1/2 tbsp. paprika
2 tsp. vege salt

1. Make soy butter.
2. Add all dry ingredients and blend well.
3. Blend in lemon juice.

   Yields: 4 Cups

Salad Dressings, Dips, and Relishes

PARSLEY DIP

1 cup soy butter (see recipe, pg. 16)
2 cloves garlic
1/4 cup fresh parsley
salt (to taste)

1. Add parsley, garlic and salt to soy butter in blender.
2. Blend well until creamy.
   Yields: 1 Cup

SUNFLOWER SEED SPREAD

1 cup sunflower seeds
2 tbsp. peppers (chopped fine)
2 tbsp. onions (chopped fine)
2 tbsp. celery (chopped fine)
1/2 cup soy butter (see recipe, pg. 16)
3 tsp. garlic powder
2 tsp. tamari sauce
1/3 cup pickle relish with juice (see recipe, pg. 77)

1. Grind sunflower seeds in blender or food processor.
2. Add all other ingredients to grounded seeds.
3. Mix well. Serve on crackers or toast.
   Yields: 3 Servings

Soul Vegetarian Cookbook

CRANBERRY -- ORANGE RELISH

1 lb. fresh cranberries	*1 cup honey*
2 large oranges	*1/8 tsp. ground cloves*

1. Wash fruit thoroughly. Squeeze juice from oranges and peel.

2. Grind cranberries and orange peeling separately in blender or food processor.

3. Mix orange juice, honey, ground orange peelings and cranberries in a 2 quart sauce pan. Cook 20 minutes on low heat.

4. Add cloves during the last 10 minutes of cooking time. Serve warm or cold with cornbread dressing.
   Yields: 4 Servings

PICKLES

2 lbs. cucumbers
5 pieces pickling spice
1/2 cup fresh dill
1 tbsp. lemon salt (level)
1 gallon water (boiling)
1/4 cup apple cider vinegar
3-4 bay leaves
1 1/2 tbsp. salt
1 gallon jar
5 cloves garlic

1. Place all ingredients in gallon jar. Pour boiling hot water over cucumbers. Let set for 3-7 days, set in dark place.
   Yields: 1 Gallon

Salad Dressings, Dips, and Relishes

SWEET PICKLE RELISH

3 1/2 lbs. cucumbers (grated large)
1/4 lb. bell peppers (chopped)
2 lbs. onions (chopped)
4 whole cloves
1 bulb garlic
1/4 lb. brown sugar
1/2 cup apple cider vinegar
juice of 3 lemons
2 tbsp. vege salt

1. Grate cucumbers and peppers on large side of grater.
2. Place remaining ingredients in a large pot and bring to a boil.
3. Add cucumbers and peppers. Remove from heat*.
4. Omit as much juice as desired. Let cool. Store in a large gallon jar in a cool place for 3-7 days. The longer they sit, the better the flavor.

*The longer ingredients are cooked, the more juice is formed.

Yields: 3 1/2 lbs.

DESSERTS

Coconut Cream Pie
Avocado Cream Pie
Banana Cream Pie
Carob Cream Pie
Apple Raisin Pecan Crunch Pie
Apple Pie
Pie Crust
Vanilla Cookie Crust
Oatmeal Crunch Crust
Strawberry Jam
Strawberry Jam Wheels
Strawberry Shortcake
Strawberry Topping
Whipped Cream Icing
Pecan Cookies
Oatmeal Coconut Cookies
Oatmeal Raisin Cookies
Carob Chip Cookies
Fruit and Nut Cookies
Spice Cookies
Banana Nut Bread
Bread Pudding
Apple Nut Cake
Carrot Loaf
Crunchy Caramel Apples
The Secretary's "Honey Crunch"
Nutty Mango Delight

COCONUT CREAM PIE

1 1/2 blocks tofu (16 oz.)
1 cup soy butter (see recipe, pg. 16)
1/2 cup cocoa cream
1-2/3 tbsp. vanilla
1 rounded tbsp. coconut (dry shredded)
1/2 cup brown sugar (blend sugar in seed grinder until powdery)
1 pie crust (see recipe, pg. 83)
2 cups cream topping. (see recipe, pg. 86)

1. Mix all ingredients in blender. Blend well.
2. Pour filling into pie crust and decorate with cream topping. (See recipe, pg. 86)
3. Freeze for 20 minutes. Serve immediately.

Yields: 3-4 Servings

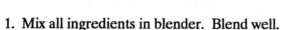

AVOCADO CREAM PIE

2 medium avocadoes
1/2 lb. honey
3 tbsp. vanilla extract
2 large bananas
2 tbsp. coconut
1 pie crust (see recipe, pg. 83)

1. Blend above ingredients together in blender.
2. Pour filling into pie crust. Spinkle coconut on top and place in refrigerator to chill.

Yields: One 9" Pie

Desserts
BANANA CREAM PIE

1/2 cup honey or 3/4 cup brown sugar
1 1/2 cups soy butter (see recipe, pg. 16)
1/2 cup soy milk (see recipe, pg. 96)
1 pie crust (see recipe, pg. 83)

8 oz. tofu
1 tbsp. vanilla extract
3 medium bananas (ripe)

1. Blend tofu with just enough milk so that mixture is very thick.
2. Add soy butter, bananas, vanilla and honey and blend until very smooth. If mixture is too thick add more soy milk.
3. Pour smooth mixture into baked pie crust and then freeze.
   Yields: One 9" Pie

CAROB CREAM PIE

1 cup soy milk (see recipe, pg. 96)
1 1/2 blocks tofu (firm)
1 1/2 cups oil
1 pie crust (see recipe, pg. 83)

2 cups honey
1 tsp. vanilla extract
2/3 cup carob powder

1. Place soy milk and honey in blender and blend well. Continue blending; a hole will form in the middle of mixture. Pour oil slowly in the center until hole closes.
2. Blend in carob powder, vanilla extract and tofu. This will make one full blender of mix.
3. Pour into pie crust in a 9" pie pan.
4. Chill and serve.
   Yields: One 9" Pie

Soul Vegetarian Cookbook

APPLE RAISIN PECAN CRUNCH PIE

9 medium apples (peeled, cored and cut into medium slices)
1 stick margarine (room temperature)
2 1/4 cups honey   *5 tbsp. vanilla*
1/2 cup pecans (chopped)   *1/4 cup raisins*
pinch vege salt   *1/2 tsp. cinnamon*
1 pie crust (see oatmeal crunch recipe, pg. 84)

1. Put apples in deep pot with margarine and simmer.
2. Stir in honey.
3. When apples are cooked slowly add vanilla and cinnamon. Let mixture cook until apples are tender. Remove from heat, stir in raisins and pecans.
Yields: One 9" Pie

APPLE PIE

12 large apples   *1 1/4 stick margarine*
1/2 tbsp. nutmeg   *2 1/2 cups honey*
3 1/2 tbsp. vanilla extract (to taste) *2 tbsp. lemon juice*
1/3 tsp. cinnamon   *1 pie crust (see recipe, pg. 83)*

1. Peel, core and slice apples, and cook with no water on low flame.
2. Add honey, nutmeg, margarine, cinnamon and let simmer.
3. Add lemon juice and stir well.
4. Pour mixture into pie crust and bake at 350 degrees for 15 minutes.
Yields: One 9" Pie

Desserts

PIE CRUST

6 cups whole wheat flour (sifted) *3 sticks margarine*
1/2 cups oil

1. Mix flour and margarine well.
2. Add oil and continue to mix.
3. Roll out dough then press into baking pan.
   (Save enough crust to cover top of pie).
4. Bake at 350 degrees for 30 minutes.

Yields: One 9" Pie

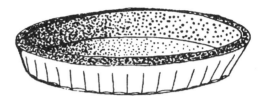

VANILLA COOKIE CRUST

2 1/2 cups whole wheat flour (sifted) *1/2 lb. honey*
1 1/2 sticks margarine *4 tbsp. vanilla extract*

1. Mix honey and margarine together thoroughly.
2. Add flour gradually until mixed thoroughly. Add vanilla extract. Make 9 large cookies and bake at 350 degrees for 12 minutes.
3. Crumble cookies and add 1/2 tsp. margarine. Moisten with a few drops of water. Put crust into 9" pie pan.
4. Add desired filling to crust. Sprinkle coconut over top and place in refrigerator to chill. Ready to serve.

Yields: One 9" Pie

Suggested pie crust for cream pies

OATMEAL CRUNCH CRUST

2 1/2 cups oatmeal
1 cup brown sugar
2 tsp. cinnamon

1/2 cup whole wheat flour
2 sticks margarine
2 tbsp. whole wheat flour

1. Add dry ingredients together, mix thoroughly. Add margarine and mix until mixture is crumbly and moist.
2. Line deep dish 9" pie pan with half of crust. Pour in filling. Top with remainder of crust.
3. Bake at 425 degrees for 30 minutes or until brown.

Yields: One 9" Pie

STRAWBERRY JAM

2 pints strawberries
2 tsp. beet juice
3 tsp. water

2 tbsp. corn starch
1/8 tsp. cloves
3/4 cup honey

1. Wash, stem and slice strawberries. Add 1 tsp. water to strawberries in a 3 quart saucepan. Heat to boiling point and turn down to medium low flame. Add 3/4 cup honey.

2. Add corn starch to 2 tbsp. cold water. Add mix gradually to strawberries, stirring constantly.
3. Stir in beet juice and cloves. Remove from heat and cool.
4. Use as filling for jam wheels, or serve with biscuits.

Yields: 3 Cups

Desserts

STRAWBERRY JAM WHEELS

WHEELS

6 cups whole wheat flour   *5 sticks soy margarine*
2 tbsp. water   *2 tsp. nutmeg*
3 cups Strawberry Jam (see recipe, pg. 84)   *1/4 cup honey*

1. Mix whole wheat flour with 4 sticks of softened margarine until desired consistency.

2. Add ice cold water to make dough rolling consistency.

3. Roll dough into 2 rectangles on a floured board until 1/4" thick.

4. Blend 1 stick softened margarine, nutmeg and 1/4 cup honey. Spread rectangles of dough with thin layer of margarine and honey mixture. Then top with layer of strawberry jam.

5. Roll filled dough, jelly roll style, sealing ends. Put both rolls in refrigerator for 30 minutes.

6. Remove rolls, slice each cookie from roll 1/2" thick.

7. Bake until edges are slightly brown at 350 degrees.

Yields: 2 Dozen

STRAWBERRY SHORTCAKE WITH WHIPPED CREAM TOPPING

3 cups brown sugar   *3 sticks margarine*
3 cups sifted whole wheat flour   *3 tbsp. vanilla extract*
1/2 cup soy milk (clabbered) (see recipe, pg. 96)

1. Mix brown sugar and margarine well until smooth and fluffy.

2. Alternate adding wheat flour and soy milk gradually.

3. Add vanilla and mix thoroughly. Bake in oven at 350 degrees for 45 minutes.

Yields: 12 Servings

STRAWBERRY TOPPING

1/2 stick margarine
1/2 cup honey
2 1/2 cups strawberries (washed and halved)
2 tbsp. vanilla extract
3 tbsp. corn starch (to thicken)

1. Combine strawberries, margarine, honey and corn starch in small pot.
2. Cook at medium heat until strawberry mixture becomes thick. Add vanilla extract.
3. Place strawberries on top of cake; add whipped cream icing.

Yields: 3 1/2 Cups

WHIPPED CREAM ICING

2 sticks chilled margarine
3 tbsp. soy milk (see recipe, pg. 96)
1 cup honey
1 tbsp. vanilla extract

1. Blend chilled margarine in blender.
2. Gradually add honey gradually. Blend on high speed. Whip until it turns fluffy white.
3. Add cold soy milk and vanilla extract. Blend well until texture is that of whipped cream.

Yields: 1 Cup

Desserts

PECAN COOKIES

2 cups honey
2 1/2 cups whole wheat flour (sifted)
1/2 cup chopped pecans
1 1/2 sticks margarine
4 tbsp. vanilla extract

1. Mix margarine and honey to a creamy, fluffy texture.
2. Add flour gradually, chopped nuts and vanilla extract. Stir well.
3. Place by spoonful on greased cookie sheet.
4. Bake at 350 degrees for 25 minutes.

Yields: 1 Dozen

OATMEAL COCONUT COOKIES

2 sticks margarine
1 tbsp. vanilla
1 3/4 cups oatmeal
2/3 cup soy milk (see recipe, pg. 96)
1 1/2 cups brown sugar
1 cup flour (sifted)
1/4 cup coconut

1. Cream margarine, sugar and vanilla together in mixing bowl.
2. Add oatmeal and coconut, adding soy milk after each dry mix. Gradually add in flour. Mix well.
3. Spoon onto greased oven pan. Flatten and bake at 350 degrees for 8 minutes.

Yields: 3 Dozen

OATMEAL RAISIN COOKIES

2 sticks margarine
2 cups oatmeal
2 cups whole wheat flour
1/4 cup soy milk

2 cups brown sugar
1/3 cup raisins
1/4 tbsp. vanilla

1. Blend together margarine and brown sugar until creamy. Add half the amount of flour and mix well.
2. Add half the amount of milk. Continue to add wheat flour and milk. Stir in vanilla. Add oatmeal and raisins. Mix well.
3. Drop by teaspoons on to greased baking sheet.
4. Bake for 15 minutes at 375 degrees.

Yields: 2 Dozen

CAROB CHIP COOKIES

1 1/2 cups brown sugar
2 cups whole wheat flour (sifted)
1/3 cup soy milk

2 sticks margarine
1 tsp. vanilla
1/2 cup carob chips

1. Cream margarine, brown sugar and vanilla together.
2. Gradually add flour, soy milk and carob chips.
3. Mix well; spoon onto greased baking sheets at 350 degrees for 8 minutes.

Yields: 3 Dozen

TIP: *Allow cookie sheets to cool completely before using for the next batch.*

Desserts

FRUIT AND NUT COOKIES

3 1/2 cups whole wheat flour
3 sticks margarine
1/2 cup soy milk
1/4 cup dates, almonds (any desired
combination -- raisins, pecans, etc.)

3 cups brown sugar
pinch of salt
2 tsp. vanilla

1. Mix sugar and margarine until smooth.

2. Add fruit and nuts, then add milk and salt. Add flour little by little until your batter is a stiff consistency.

3. Drop by spoonful and press into desired shape. Bake at 325 degrees for 10 - 15 minutes or until brown on bottom.

Yields: 2 - 2 1/2 Dozen

SPICE COOKIES

3 1/4 cups flour
2 tbsp. tahini
2 tbsp. vanilla extract
1 level tbsp. nutmeg
pinch of salt

3 cups brown sugar
1 tbsp. molasses
1 tbsp. cinnamon
2 sticks margarine
1/2 cup clabbered soy milk
(see recipe, pg. 96)

1. Mix together tahini, molasses and vanilla in large mixing bowl. Cream margarine and tahini mixture; whip until smooth.

2. Add to mixture brown sugar, cinnamon, nutmeg and salt; blend well. Stir in flour and milk until batter is smooth. Drop by spoonfuls on greased cookie sheet and lightly press into desired shape.

3. Bake at 350 degrees approximately 10 minutes or until brown on bottom.

Yields: 3 Dozen

Soul Vegetarian Cookbook

BANANA NUT BREAD

3 sticks margarine

4 cups whole wheat flour (sifted)

1 tsp. lemon rind (grated)

1/2 cup soy pulp*

1 cup nuts (chopped)**

2 1/2 cups honey

1/4 tsp. salt

3 tbsp. hot water

4 cups banana pulp (mashed)

1/2 cup raisins (chopped)

1. Combine dry ingredients in large bowl. Stir well.

2. In separate bowl, mix margarine and honey together. Add half of banana pulp to mixture. Mix well.

3. Add half of dry ingredients. Continue to mix well. Add remaining banana pulp and remaining dry ingredients. Beat for 10 minutes.

4. Raisins, nuts, lemon rind and hot water can be added last. Stir in well.

5. Pour mixture into oiled, floured loaf pan. Bake at 300 degrees for one hour or until toothpick inserted in center comes out clean.

Yields: 12 Servings

* See Helpful Cooking Hints

** Your choice of nuts

Desserts

BREAD PUDDING

2 sticks margarine
1 loaf bread (see recipe, pg. 10)
1 tsp. cinnamon

1 tsp. nutmeg
1 cup brown sugar
1 cup soy milk

1. Cream margarine and sugar.
2. Cut up bread in small pieces and add to mixture, adding milk as you add bread.
3. Add nutmeg and cinnamon. Mix well.
4. Place in square pan. Bake for 1 hour at 350 degrees.

Yields: 8 Servings

APPLE NUT CAKE

3 cups whole wheat flour
2 tsp. cinnamon
1 tsp. vanilla flavor
1 cup apple juice
3 sticks margarine

3 cups brown sugar
1/2 tsp. salt
1/2 cup raisins
1 1/2 cups apples (diced)
1/2 cup nuts (chopped)

1. Preheat oven to 350 degrees. Grease and flour a 13" x 9" pan.
2. In large bowl, combine first 7 ingredients. Beat with mixer 3 minutes at medium speed or by hand until smooth. Stir in apples, nuts and raisins.

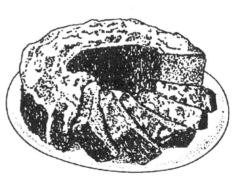

3. Pour into greased, floured pan. Bake 30-40 minutes or until toothpick inserted in center comes out clean.

Yields: 8 Servings

Soul Vegetarian Cookbook

CARROT LOAF

1 1/2 cups sugar

3 cups carrot pulp (from juiced carrots)

1 cup soy milk (see recipe pg. 96)

1 lb. flour

2 sticks margarine

1 tsp. cinnamon

1 tsp. nutmeg

1. Put sugar, margarine and flour in bowl. Mix with hands until flaky.

2. Add carrot pulp, cinnamon, nutmeg and milk until soft.

3. Place in loaf pan for 1 hour or until sides leave pan. Bake at 350 degrees.

Yields: 8 Servings

CRUNCHY CARAMEL APPLES

1/3 lb. brown sugar

2 tbsp. margarine

3 tsp. water

1/2 tsp. nutmeg

1 1/2 lbs. (3 large) red apples
   (pared and sliced into rings)

2 tbsp. olive oil

1/2 cup walnuts

1/4 cup golden raisins

dash of vege salt

1. Saute walnuts in olive oil and margarine in large skillet until lightly toasted. Remove from pan.

2. Brown apple rings on both sides until tender.

3. Place apples and nuts in shallow serving dish. Keep warm.

4. Combine remaining ingredients in skillet.

5. Stir and heat until brown sugar dissolves and boils. Pour over apples and nuts. Serve warm.

Yields: 6 Servings

Desserts

THE SECRETARY'S "HONEY CRUNCH"

2 cups honey

3/4 cup toasted wheat germ

1 cup peanuts, roasted and crushed

3/4 cup tahini

1/2 cup coconut

1/2 tsp. rum flavor

1. In a large pot, allow honey to come to a boil. Reduce flame and simmer 3 to 4 minutes.

2. Remove from heat, add tahini and rum flavor and mix well.

3. Add dry ingredients and mix well.

4. Pour hot mixture into a slightly oiled oven pan. Spread with a large wooden spoon or spatula. Let cool.

5. Cut with knife and place in 1 1/2 size candy paper cups.

Yields: 30 Pieces

NUTTY MANGO DELIGHT

1/2 cup nuts of your choice

1/2 qt. vanilla soy ice cream

honey (to taste)

1 mango (diced)

1/4 cup raisins

1. Place mango in serving dish. Fold in raisins and honey.

2. Top with nuts and soy ice cream.

Yields: 1 Serving

BEVERAGES

Soy Milk

Hot Carob Drink

Carrot Drink

Lemon Mist

Cafe Fenugreek

Peanut Honey Shake

Seventh Heaven Vegetable Juice

Soybean Coffee

Soul Vegetarian Cookbook

SOY MILK

1/2 cup soy flour (sifted)   *3 cups water*

1. Combine flour and 2 cups water in bowl to form a paste.
2. Place remaining water in small pot. Add paste. Stir constantly over low heat. Allow mixture to come to a roaring boil.
3. Cook until skim appears on top. Remove skim and strain milk.
4. Cool before serving.

   Yields: 2 1/2 Cups

HOT CAROB DRINK

1/2 cup carob powder   *3 tsp. honey*
3 cups soy milk (see recipe above)   *1 tbsp. vanilla*
3 tbsp. soy butter (see recipe, pg. 16)

1. Place all ingredients in a blender and blend.
2. Heat and serve.

   Yields: 4 - 5 Servings

CARROT DRINK

2 lbs. carrots   *1/2 cup honey*
1/2 cup grated coconut   *1 tsp. nutmeg*
1 cup soy milk (see recipe above)   *2 cups water*

1. Pre-wash and scrape carrots until clean. Juice carrots.
2. Add remaining ingredients to carrot juice and blend. Can be served with ice.

   Yields: 3 Servings

Beverages

LEMON MIST

2 cups water
1/2 cup honey

juice of 4 medium lemons
5 ice cubes

1. In blender, blend lemon juice and honey well.
2. Add ice cubes and blend slightly for slush-like consistency.

Yields: 1-8 Oz. Serving

CAFE FENUGREEK

2 tbsp. fenugreek (powdered)
1 tbsp. carob powder
4 1/4 cups boiling water
honey (to taste)

7 tbsp. sesame seed paste
1 tsp. molasses
1/4 tsp. cinnamon
1 tbsp. vanilla flavor (optional)

1. In a medium pot, add boiling water to fenugreek powder. Let stand for 5 minutes or more. Strain.
2. In a large mixing bowl mix sesame seed paste, carob powder, cinnamon, vanilla flavor and molasses until creamy.
3. Gradually add hot fenugreek water (not pulp) and blend well.
4. Add honey to taste.

The use of a blender will make a smoother drink.

Yields: 2 Servings

PEANUT HONEY SHAKE

1/3 cup creamy peanut butter
honey (to taste)

1/8 tsp. vanilla flavor
14 oz. water

In blender, blend all ingredients until creamy. Chill with ice cubes and serve.

Yields: 2 Servings

SEVENTH HEAVEN VEGETABLE JUICE

2 lbs. carrots
1/2 cucumber
1/2 celery stalk
1/4 small beet

1/2 small tomato
4 oz. fresh parsley
1/2 small bell pepper

Wash all vegetables well and juice in an electric juicer. Ready to drink.

Yields: 1 Serving

SOYBEAN COFFEE

1/2 cup ground roasted soybeans   1 qt. water

1. **To Prepare Beans**
    a. Spread dry yellow beans (picked and cleaned) in a shallow pan.

    b. Bake in oven at 200 degrees for several hours until beans are a dark brown coffee color.

    c. Grind soybeans in a hand grinder to crack beans.

    d. Store in glass jar with tight lid to retain flavor.

2. **To Prepare Coffee**
    a. Place the prepared soybeans in a pot with 1 qt. of water.

    b. Bring to a boil and let simmer for 20 minutes. Let steep.

    The longer steeping time will give a richer flavor to the coffee. The coffee will be good the next day; just reheat and serve black or with honey and nut creams.

    Yields: 1 Quart

SUGGESTED MENUS

BREAKFAST

- Oatmeal with Honey, Toast, Scrambled Tofu.

- Pancakes with Honey or Toast and Jelly, Scrambled Tofu, Bulgar Patties.

- Chopped Apples and Bananas with Toasted Wheatgerm topped with Honey, Margarine and Vanilla flavor. Sprinkle Coconut on top.

- Citrus Fruits Salad: Chopped Oranges, Grapefruit with Wheatgerm and Coconut sprinkled on top.

- Biscuits with Gravy, Rice, Scrambled Tofu.

- Smothered Hash Brown Potatoes with Onions, Scrambled Tofu, Sprouts and Tomatoes.

LUNCH - DINNER

- Spaghetti, Cole Slaw, Battered Tofu, Vegetable, Salad.

- Beet Loaf, Greens, Lettuce/Tomato/Cucumber Salad, Candied Carrots.

- Protein Roast, Mashed Potatoes, Stringbeans, Salad.

- Bar-B-Que Twists, Potato Salad, Vegetable Salad.

- Avocado Salad, Super Live Salad, Carrot Supreme, Whole Wheat Crackers.

- Chickpeas over Rice, Steamed Broccoli, Salad, Cornbread.

- Baked Potatoes, Tossed Salad, Beets, Sauteed Spinach with Onions.

- Garvey Burger Loaf, Hebrew Rice, Yellow Squash, Salad.

- Stuffed Bell Peppers, Garden Salad, Tomato and Avocado Slices.

- Vegetable Chili, Salad, Cornbread.

Suggested Menus

*Important Food Supplements
Needed For A Balanced Diet*

BREWERS YEAST

Contains the complete vitamin B complex.

5 -7 Months: 1/2 tsp. with Breakfast

7 Months - 3 Years: 1 1/2 tsp. with Breakfast and Dinner

3 - 12 Years: 1 tbsp. with Dinner

12 Years - Adult: 1 Heaping tbsp. with Dinner

SESAME SEEDS (GROUND)

An excellent source of calcium and phosphorus.

Babies and Children: 3 - 4 tsp. Daily

Teens and Adults: 1/2 cup Daily

Expecting Mothers: 1 cup Daily

BLACKSTRAP MOLASSES

An excellent source of iron and calcium.

5 Months - 3 Years: 1 tsp. 3 times a day with water

3 Years - Adult: 1 tbsp. with 1/2 cup water Daily

SOY MILK

An excellent source of calcium and protein.

Babies and Children: 2 times Daily

Teens and Adults: 1 8 oz. glass Daily

Soul Vegetarian Cookbook

PARSLEY
Rich in vitamin A.
Babies and Children: 2 Sprigs Daily
Teens and Adults: 3 Sprigs Daily

WHEATGERM
High in vitamin E and iron.
5 Months - 6 Years: 2 tsp. Daily
6 Years - Adult: 3 tsp. Daily

BEAN SPOUTS
Very rich in vitamins B and C.
Put them in your diet as often as possible.
Alfalfa sprouts are most popular and most nutritious.

CHICK PEAS AND SOY BEANS
One of the highest forms of protein available.
One serving 2 times a week.
(Served with brown rice makes a complete protein meal.)

KELP
High in calcium.
5 Months -1 Year: 1/2 tsp. Daily
1- 6 Years: 1 tsp. Daily
6 Years - Adult: 1 Tbsp. Daily

Consistency is the key for supplements to work!

THE DIVINE DIET

The Divine Diet of the African Hebrew Israelite Community of Jerusalem consists of fruits, vegetables and nuts. This diet is recommended for pregnant women and nursing mothers. It is also a preventive measure against illness, and is necessary if you are seeking perfect health and a long life.

From the **VEGETARIAN TIMES,** August 1989

"Natural Foods. Owned by a group of Hebrew Israelites. Food is wonderful and completely vegan. Gluten Bar-B-Que Twist on Whole Wheat Bun, or Roast with Gravy, Veggie Gyros. And you must try the Peanut Butter Ice Cream; It a prized and secret recipe. Friendly service. Reservations for parties larger than eight. Open daily, but breakfast is served only Tuesday through Saturday"

Soul Vegetarian Restaurant
879-A Ralph Abernathy Blvd. SW, Atlanta, GA 30310 - (404) *752-5194*

Vegetarian International
652 North Highland - Atlanta, GA 30306 - (404) 874-0145

Soul Vegetarian East
205 B. 75th St. - Chicago, IL 60619 - (312) 224-0104

Soul Vegetarian Restaurant & Exodus Carry-Out
2606 Georgia Ave. NW - Washington, DC 20001 - (202) EAT-SOUL *(328-7685)*

Soul Vegetarian Gourmet
9185 Central Avenue – Capitol Heights, MD 20743 – (301) 324-6900

Soul Vegetarian Restaurant
2240 Lee Road - Cleveland Heights, OH 44118 - (216) 932-0588

Ta'am HaChaim (Taste of Life) – Tel Aviv
60 Ben Yehuda - Tel Aviv, Israel - 011- 972-3-620-3151

Ta'am HaChaim (Taste of Life) - Beersheba
Migdahl HaraKhavets 6 - (Train Tower- #6) Beersheba, Israel - 011-972-07-665-0859

Soul Vegetarian International
1 DA Estate Diamond, Christiansted - St. Croix, U.S.VI. - (340) 778-4080

Soul Vegetarian Restaurant
Abeka LaPaz - Ghana (2 Blocks Left of Mobile Station) at LaPaz Junction across from Lucapp

Source of Life Juice Bar
(Located in Everlasting Life Health Complex & Organic Market)
2928 Georgia Avenue, NW - Washington, DC 20001 - (202) 232-1700

Return to Eden
383 Alsreton Road; Nottingham, NG75LT - London, England - 011-5-970-4315

Notes